2025
Python Programming

Coding, Projects, and Problem-Solving Automation

By: Dr. Evelyn Harper

Table of Contents

Introduction

In a world where technology drives innovation, Python has emerged as one of the most versatile and accessible programming languages. From automating mundane tasks to developing cutting-edge applications, Python's simplicity and power make it a top choice for beginners and professionals alike. Welcome to *Python Programming: Coding, Projects, and Problem Solving*, your comprehensive guide to mastering the art of Python programming through hands-on learning, real-world projects, and strategic problem-solving.

Whether you are a complete novice looking to dip your toes into the world of programming or an experienced coder aiming to sharpen your skills, this book is designed with you in mind. Python's intuitive syntax and extensive library support create a perfect platform to explore programming concepts, build functional applications, and solve complex problems efficiently.

Why Python?

Python is more than just a programming language; it's a tool that empowers you to bring your ideas to life. Its versatility spans across diverse fields like data analysis, web development, artificial intelligence, and automation. Python is used by tech giants such as Google, Netflix, and NASA, but it's also beginner-friendly, making it an ideal first language for aspiring programmers. This book harnesses Python's potential to provide you with a solid foundation and the confidence to tackle any coding challenge.

What This Book Offers

In this book, you will find:

- **Clear and Concise Explanations**: Learn Python programming concepts step-by-step, with clear explanations and practical examples that demystify complex topics.
- **Engaging Projects**: Apply your knowledge to build exciting projects, ranging from simple scripts to more advanced applications, giving you real-world experience and a portfolio to showcase.
- **Problem-Solving Strategies**: Develop a logical and analytical mindset to approach coding challenges effectively, with detailed walkthroughs and best practices.
- **Hands-On Exercises**: Reinforce your learning with exercises and challenges designed to test your understanding and boost your confidence.

Who Is This Book For?

- **Beginners**: If you have no prior experience in programming, this book will guide you from the basics to advanced concepts in a structured and accessible way.
- **Students and Educators**: Ideal for those studying Python in school or university, this book serves as a valuable companion to formal education.
- **Professionals**: If you're looking to automate tasks, build tools, or transition into tech-driven roles, this book equips you with the skills needed to succeed.

A Journey of Discovery

This book is not just about writing code; it's about cultivating a mindset of curiosity, creativity, and persistence. With each chapter, you'll unlock new possibilities and gain confidence in your abilities as a programmer. The projects and challenges will inspire you to think critically, experiment boldly, and continuously refine your skills.

So, are you ready to embark on this exciting journey? Let's dive into the world of Python programming, where every line of code is a step closer to transforming your ideas into reality. Together, we will explore, create, and solve — one project at a time.

Chapter 1: Python Unleashed: Why It's the Language of the Future

In the fast-paced world of technology, choosing the right programming language can be the key to unlocking limitless opportunities. Among hundreds of programming languages, one stands out not only for its simplicity but also for its unmatched versatility—Python. Whether you're an aspiring developer, a data scientist, or someone just beginning their coding journey, Python offers something for everyone.

This chapter will explore why Python has become the language of choice for millions of developers worldwide. We'll delve into its unique features, industry adoption, and the groundbreaking opportunities it unlocks for anyone willing to learn.

A Brief History of Python

Before we dive into Python's strengths, let's take a quick look at its origins. Python was created by Guido van Rossum in 1991, with a clear vision to make programming accessible, intuitive, and fun. Unlike other languages that were overly complex or niche-specific, Python was designed with simplicity and readability at its core. Over the decades, Python has evolved into a robust, multi-paradigm language powering some of the world's most advanced technologies.

Why Python Stands Out

Python's success can be attributed to several defining characteristics:

1. **Readability**: Python's syntax resembles plain English, making it incredibly beginner-friendly. Developers can focus on solving problems rather than deciphering complicated code.
2. **Versatility**: Python is a general-purpose language, excelling in diverse domains like web development, data science, automation, artificial intelligence, and game development.
3. **Vast Libraries and Frameworks**: Python boasts a rich ecosystem of libraries and frameworks (e.g., Pandas, Django, TensorFlow) that simplify complex tasks.
4. **Community Support**: With a global community of developers, Python users have access to countless tutorials, forums, and open-source projects to accelerate their learning.

Industry Applications

Python's widespread adoption is a testament to its versatility. Here are some real-world applications that showcase Python's power:

1. **Web Development**: Frameworks like Django and Flask enable developers to build robust web applications with minimal effort.
2. **Data Science and Machine Learning**: Python is the backbone of data-driven industries, thanks to libraries like NumPy, Pandas, and Scikit-learn.
3. **Artificial Intelligence**: From natural language processing to computer vision, Python powers advanced AI applications.
4. **Automation**: Python scripts simplify tedious tasks, boosting productivity in IT operations and beyond.

5. **Game Development**: Libraries like Pygame make game development accessible even to beginners.
6. **Finance and FinTech**: Python is widely used in algorithmic trading, financial analysis, and risk management.

Python in Numbers

- **Most Popular Language**: According to the TIOBE Index, Python consistently ranks as the most popular programming language globally.
- **Employer Demand**: Python developers are in high demand, with average salaries exceeding those of other programming roles.
- **Adoption by Tech Giants**: Companies like Google, Netflix, Facebook, and NASA rely on Python for mission-critical applications.

Python vs. Other Languages

Let's compare Python with other programming languages to understand its advantages:

Feature	Python	Java	C++	JavaScript
Learning Curve	Easy	Moderate	Steep	Moderate
Readability	High	Moderate	Low	Moderate
Applications	Versatile	Versatile	Performance-heavy	Web-focused
Libraries & Frameworks	Extensive	Extensive	Moderate	Extensive
Developer Community	Large	Large	Medium	Large

Why Python is the Language of the Future

Python is not just a language; it's an ecosystem that thrives on innovation. Here's why it's poised to lead the future of technology:

1. **AI and Machine Learning Revolution**: Python's simplicity and library support make it the top choice for AI and ML development.

2. **Data Explosion**: With the rise of big data, Python has become indispensable for data analysis and visualization.
3. **Cloud Computing**: Python's compatibility with cloud platforms (e.g., AWS, Google Cloud) ensures its relevance in modern IT infrastructure.
4. **IoT and Robotics**: Python is increasingly used in Internet of Things (IoT) and robotics applications due to its ease of use and rapid prototyping capabilities.
5. **Beginner Appeal**: As more people enter the tech field, Python's beginner-friendly nature ensures a steady influx of new developers.

Quick Start Guide: Getting Python Up and Running

Let's get you started with Python in just a few steps:

1. **Download Python**: Visit python.org and download the latest version of Python.
2. **Install an IDE**: Use beginner-friendly tools like PyCharm or Visual Studio Code.
3. **Write Your First Script**: Open a Python file and type:

python

print("Hello, World!")

Run your code and watch Python in action

Python's Versatility and Simplicity: The Perfect Combination

Python is renowned for its versatility and simplicity, two characteristics that make it the go-to programming language for developers, hobbyists, and industry professionals alike. These traits allow Python to be used in a variety of domains while remaining accessible even to beginners. Let's delve into what makes Python so versatile and simple and explore the real-world applications that set it apart.

Simplicity: The Core of Python's Appeal

One of Python's greatest strengths is its simplicity, which comes from a design philosophy that prioritizes readability and ease of use. This makes Python the perfect choice for both beginners and experienced developers alike.

Let's talk about **readable syntax**, one of the reasons Python is so beginner-friendly. Python's syntax is clean and intuitive—so much so that it often feels like reading plain English. For example, consider this simple snippet of code:

'Imagine you want to calculate the sum of two numbers. You could write it like this:

First, assign the value 10 to a variable named a. Then, assign the value 20 to another variable, b. Finally, add these two variables together and print the result. Here's what that looks like in Python:

a = 10b = 20

print (a + b)

1. **Low Barrier to Entry**: Python eliminates unnecessary complexities like managing memory or specifying variable types, allowing beginners to focus

on learning programming concepts instead of wrestling with syntax.

2. **Robust Standard Library**: Python comes with a vast standard library that simplifies tasks ranging from file manipulation to network communication. This reduces the need for external dependencies and additional learning.

3. **Cross-Platform Compatibility**: Python runs seamlessly on major operating systems like Windows, macOS, and Linux. Code written on one platform often requires little to no modification to work on another.

Versatility: One Language, Endless Possibilities

Python's versatility lies in its ability to adapt to a wide range of use cases. It is a general-purpose language that thrives in virtually every technological domain.

1. **Multi-Paradigm Support**: Python supports multiple programming paradigms, including procedural, object-oriented, and functional programming. This flexibility allows developers to choose the approach best suited for their projects.

2. **Diverse Libraries and Frameworks**: Python's rich ecosystem of libraries and frameworks expands its capabilities. Whether you're building a web application or analyzing data, there's likely a Python library that fits your needs.

3. **Scalability**: Python scales effortlessly from small scripts to enterprise-level applications. It can be used for prototyping, and as the project grows, Python remains relevant thanks to its powerful libraries and integrations.

Real-World Applications of Python

Python's combination of simplicity and versatility has led to its widespread adoption in numerous industries. Here are some key areas where Python excels:

1. Artificial Intelligence (AI) and Machine Learning (ML)

Python is a cornerstone of AI and ML development, thanks to its extensive libraries and frameworks that simplify complex computations.

- **Popular Libraries**:
    - **TensorFlow** and **PyTorch** for deep learning.
    - **Scikit-learn** for traditional machine learning models.
    - **NLTK** and **SpaCy** for natural language processing.
- **Applications**:
    - Recommendation systems (e.g., Netflix, Amazon).
    - Image recognition and computer vision (e.g., self-driving cars).
    - Chatbots and virtual assistants (e.g., Siri, Alexa).
- **Example**: A Python script can train a machine learning model to classify emails as spam or not spam using a few lines of code:

python

from sklearn.ensemble import RandomForestClassifier

```
model = RandomForestClassifier()
model.fit(X_train, y_train)
```

2. Web Development

Python powers some of the internet's most popular websites and applications through its web frameworks.

- **Popular Frameworks**:
    - **Django**: A high-level framework for building scalable web applications.
    - **Flask**: A lightweight framework ideal for smaller projects or API development.
    - **FastAPI**: A modern framework optimized for speed and asynchronous functionality.
- **Applications**:
    - E-commerce platforms (e.g., Shopify backend integrations).
    - Social media sites (e.g., Instagram uses Django).
    - RESTful APIs for mobile and web apps.

Example: Building a simple web app with Flask:

- To create a simple web application using Flask in Python, start by importing the Flask class from the flask module. Then, initialize the app by creating an instance of the Flask class. Define a route for the homepage by using the @app.route("/") decorator, followed by a function named home that returns a welcome message, such as "Welcome to my Python-powered website!" Finally, check if the script is being run directly by using the if __name__ == "__main__": condition and start the app with the app. Run

12

(debug=True) command, enabling debug mode for easier development and troubleshooting.

3. Automation and Scripting

Python simplifies tedious and repetitive tasks, making it an invaluable tool for automation.

- **Popular Libraries**:
    - **Selenium**: Automates web browser interactions.
    - **PyAutoGUI**: Controls mouse and keyboard actions for desktop automation.
    - **OS and Shutil**: Built-in libraries for file and system management.
- **Applications**:
    - Data entry and report generation.
    - Automated testing for software.
    - File organization and backup systems.
- **Example**: Automating file renaming in a directory:

To rename files in a folder using Python, first import the os module. Then, specify the path to your folder by assigning it to the folder_path variable. Use a for loop to iterate over each file in the folder, which is retrieved by os.list dir (folder_path). For each file, use the os.rename() method to rename it. The new name for each file is constructed by combining the folder path with a new name pattern, such as "file_" followed by the file's index, and ending with the .txt extension. This will rename all the files in the specified folder sequentially.

4. Data Analysis and Visualization

Python dominates the field of data science, enabling users to extract insights from raw data.

- **Popular Libraries**:
    - **Pandas**: For data manipulation and analysis.
    - **NumPy**: For numerical computations.
    - **Matplotlib** and **Seaborn**: For creating stunning visualizations.
- **Applications**:
    - Financial trend analysis.
    - Customer behavior prediction.
    - Scientific research.
- **Example**: Creating a simple data visualization:

Let's explore how to visualize revenue growth over time with a simple line plot using Python. We'll use two powerful tools for this: pandas and mat plot lib, both essential for working with data and creating visualizations.

Here's how it works:

Imagine starting with a dataset that includes two main pieces of information—years and corresponding revenue figures. For example, you might have years like 2020, 2021, and 2022 alongside their respective revenue numbers. With Python, we can organize this data into a structured format called a Data Frame, which is perfect for analysis and visualization.

Once your data is ready, you can create a line plot to represent it visually. The horizontal axis (x-axis) will show the years, and the vertical axis (y-axis) will represent the revenue. Adding a clear title to the plot provides context, making it easy to interpret.

When you bring everything together and display the plot, you'll see a smooth line that connects the data points, illustrating how revenue has changed over time. This simple yet powerful approach shows how Python transforms raw numbers into meaningful visuals, making it easier to spot trends and gain insights at a glance.

5. Gaming and Entertainment

Python has a growing presence in game development and creative industries.

- **Popular Libraries**:
    - **Pygame**: Simplifies 2D game development.
    - **Unity (with Python integration)**: For game scripting.
- **Applications**:
    - Developing educational games for kids.
    - Creating 2D arcade games.
    - Building interactive storytelling experiences.
- **Example**: Creating a basic game loop with Pygame:

Quick-Start Guide to Setting Up Python in Under 10 Minutes

Getting started with Python is incredibly simple and can be done in a few easy steps. Whether you're using Windows, macOS, or Linux, this quick-start guide will have you up and running with Python in less than 10 minutes.

Step 1: Download Python

1. Visit the official Python website: <u>python.org</u>.
2. Click on the **Downloads** tab, and the site will automatically detect your operating system (Windows, macOS, or Linux).
3. Download the latest stable version (e.g., Python 3.x.x).

Step 2: Install Python

1. **Windows Users**:
   - Run the downloaded .exe file.
   - In the installer window, check the box that says **"Add Python to PATH"** (this is crucial for easy access).
   - Click **Install Now** and let the setup complete.
2. **macOS Users**:
   - Open the downloaded .pkg file.
   - Follow the installer prompts to complete the installation.
   - Alternatively, use **Homebrew** by running:

   bash

   brew install python

3. **Linux Users**:
   - Open a terminal and type:

   bash

   sudo apt update
   sudo apt install python3

   - Verify the installation by typing:

bash

python3 --version

Step 3: Install an IDE or Text Editor

An Integrated Development Environment (IDE) or a text editor helps you write and manage Python code efficiently.

- **Beginner-Friendly Choices**:
    - **Thonny**: A simple IDE specifically designed for Python beginners.
    - **IDLE**: Comes bundled with Python and is a good starting point.
- **Popular IDEs for Advanced Users**:
    - **PyCharm**: Feature-rich and powerful.
    - **Visual Studio Code**: Lightweight and highly customizable.

Step 4: Test Your Installation

1. Open a terminal or command prompt.
2. Type python (or python3 on Linux/Mac) and press Enter.
3. You'll see the Python interpreter start with a >>> prompt.
4. Test it by typing:

   python

   print("Hello, World!")

5. If you see Hello, World! printed, your Python setup is ready to go.

Step 5: Install Essential Libraries

For most projects, you'll need additional libraries. Use Python's built-in package manager, pip, to install them:

bash

pip install numpy pandas matplotlib

These libraries will prepare you for data analysis, visualization, and other tasks.

Why Learning Python Today is a Game-Changer for Your Career

Python isn't just another programming language; it's a transformative tool that can open doors to a wide range of lucrative and exciting opportunities. Here's why learning Python today could be the most impactful decision for your career:

1. In-Demand Skill in a Booming Job Market

Python consistently ranks as one of the most in-demand programming languages across industries. A growing number of companies, from startups to tech giants like Google, Netflix, and NASA, rely on Python for critical projects.

- **Job Opportunities**:
  - Data Analyst
  - Machine Learning Engineer
  - Software Developer
  - Web Developer
  - Automation Engineer

- **High Salaries**: Python developers often earn competitive salaries, with the average Python programmer in the U.S. earning over $110,000 annually.

2. Versatility Across Industries

Python's applications span a vast array of fields, making it a versatile skill that can be adapted to various career paths. Whether you're interested in AI, data science, web development, finance, or even game development, Python is your gateway.

- **Examples of Real-World Use**:
    - Building predictive models in healthcare.
    - Creating e-commerce platforms for retail businesses.
    - Automating workflows in finance and banking.

3. Rapid Prototyping and Problem Solving

Python allows you to bring ideas to life quickly. Its simplicity and vast library support make it ideal for building prototypes, automating repetitive tasks, and solving real-world problems.

- **Why This Matters**:
    - Impress employers or clients with quick turnarounds on projects.
    - Transition seamlessly from concept to deployment.

4. Gateway to Emerging Technologies

Python dominates cutting-edge fields like artificial intelligence, machine learning, and data science. Learning Python equips you with the tools to dive into these high-growth areas.

- **Why It's Important**:
    - AI and machine learning are reshaping industries, from marketing to healthcare.
    - Data-driven decision-making is becoming the norm, making Python-based data analysis an invaluable skill.

5. A Supportive and Active Community

Python has one of the largest and most active developer communities in the world. No matter your skill level, you'll find forums, tutorials, and online resources to help you succeed.

- **What This Means for You**:
    - Quick solutions to coding challenges.
    - Access to free resources like open-source libraries and GitHub projects.
    - Opportunities to contribute and grow as a developer.

6. Future-Proof Your Career

Technology is evolving rapidly, but Python's adaptability ensures its relevance in the foreseeable future. By learning Python now, you're equipping yourself with a skill that will continue to pay dividends for years to come.

Motivational Takeaway

Imagine this: With just a few weeks of dedication, you could write a program that automates your daily tasks, develop a web application that earns passive income, or create an AI-powered tool that solves real-world problems. Learning Python is more than just acquiring a skill—it's investing in a future where you have the power to innovate, create, and thrive in a tech-driven world.

So why wait? The time to learn Python is now, and the possibilities are endless.

Chapter 2: Python Basics Reinvented: Learning by Doing

Programming isn't just about memorizing syntax—it's about solving problems and creating solutions. This chapter takes a unique, hands-on approach to learning Python basics by diving into practical exercises and real-world scenarios. By focusing on "learning by doing," you'll build confidence in coding and gain a deeper understanding of Python fundamentals.

We'll cover Python's essential building blocks in this chapter, but instead of lengthy explanations, you'll learn by working on exercises, projects, and challenges that solidify these concepts.

2.1 Getting Started: Writing Your First Python Program

Let's begin with the simplest program that every programmer writes when learning a new language: printing "Hello, World!" to the screen.

1. Open your IDE or terminal.
2. Type the following:

   python

   print("Hello, World!")

3. Run the code. You've just written your first Python program!

Now, let's make it interactive. Modify the program to ask for your name:

22

python

```python
name = input("What is your name? ")
print(f"Hello, {name}! Welcome to Python.")
```

Challenge: Modify the program to ask for the user's age and calculate the year they'll turn 100.

2.2 Variables and Data Types: The Foundation of Python

Variables store data that your program can manipulate. In Python, you don't need to declare variable types—they're assigned automatically based on the value.

Examples:

To define different types of variables in Python, start by assigning an integer value to a variable. For example, you can set age to 25. To define a floating-point number, assign a value like 5.9 to the variable height. For a string, assign a value in quotation marks, such as "Alice", to the variable name. Lastly, to define a boolean value, set a variable like is_student to True or False, depending on the condition you want to represent.

Hands-On Exercise:

- Write a program that calculates the area of a rectangle:

To calculate the area of a rectangle in Python, first prompt the user to input the length by using the input() function and convert the input to a floating-point number using float().

Store this value in a variable called length. Next, prompt the user to enter the width in the same way and store the value in the variable width. To calculate the area, multiply the length by the width and assign the result to the variable area. Finally, display the calculated area using the print() function, formatting the message to include the value of area.

Challenge: Extend the program to calculate the perimeter.

2.3 Control Structures: Making Decisions

In Python, you can use if-else statements to make decisions based on conditions, and loops like for and while to repeat actions.

For an example of an **if-else** statement, you can prompt the user to input the temperature as an integer. If the temperature is greater than 30, print "It's hot outside!" Otherwise, print "The weather is nice."

For a **for loop** example, you can use the for statement with the range() function to iterate over a sequence of numbers. In this case, the loop will run five times, printing "This is line" followed by the current loop iteration number.

For a **hands-on exercise**, you can write a program to check if a number is even or odd. First, prompt the user to enter a number, then check if the number is divisible by 2 using the modulus operator (%). If the result is zero, print "The number is even." Otherwise, print "The number is odd."

Challenge: Modify the program to check if a number is prime.

2.4 Collections: Lists, Tuples, and Dictionaries

In Python, you can store and manage collections of data in several powerful ways, including lists, tuples, and dictionaries.

A **list** is a collection of items that can be modified. For example, you can create a list called fruits with the items "apple," "banana," and "cherry." You can then add a new item, "orange," to the list using the .append() method. Finally, you can print the list to see the updated collection.

A **tuple** is similar to a list, but it is immutable, meaning its items cannot be changed once defined. For example, you can create a tuple called colors with the values "red," "green," and "blue." To access an element in a tuple, you can reference it by its index, such as colors[0] to print "red."

A **dictionary** stores data as key-value pairs. For instance, you can create a dictionary called student with keys like "name," "age," and "grade," each paired with corresponding values. To access a specific value, like the student's name, you can use the key student["name"].

For a **hands-on exercise**, you can write a program that stores and displays a student's details. First, prompt the user to input the student's name, age, and grade, storing these values in a dictionary. Finally, print the dictionary to display the student's details.

Challenge: Add functionality to update the grade.

2.5 Functions: Reusing Code

In Python, **functions** are reusable blocks of code that perform specific tasks. To **define a function**, use the def keyword, followed by the function name and any parameters in parentheses. For example, a function called greet takes one parameter, name, and prints a greeting like "Hello, [name]!" To **call a function**, simply use the function name and pass in the required argument, such as greet("Alice").

For a **hands-on exercise**, you can write a function to calculate the **factorial** of a number. Define the function factorial that takes a number n as an argument. If n is 0 or 1, the function returns 1. Otherwise, it recursively calls itself, multiplying n by the factorial of n - 1. After defining the function, prompt the user to input a number and print the result, like "The factorial of [number] is [result]."

For a **challenge**, you could write a function to check if a string is a **palindrome**, meaning it reads the same forward and backward.

Python also allows you to **interact with users** through **input and output**. For example, to **write to a file**, open the file in write mode using with open("output.txt", "w") and use file.write() to write content. To **read from a file**, open the file in read mode with with open("output.txt", "r"), and use file.read() to display the contents.

For another **hands-on exercise**, you can write a program that saves a user's to-do list to a file. You would prompt the user for input, store the tasks, and then save them to a text file.

Challenge: Add functionality to load and display the to-do list.

2.7 Debugging: Learning from Mistakes

Errors are inevitable when coding, but Python's error messages make it easy to debug.

Common Errors:

- **SyntaxError**: Mistyping a keyword or forgetting a colon.
- **TypeError**: Using incompatible data types.
- **NameError**: Using an undefined variable.

Hands-On Debugging Exercise:

The program starts by attempting to print a message prompting the user to enter two numbers for addition, but there's a missing closing quotation mark in the print statement. To fix it, add the missing quotation mark at the end of the string.

Next, the program attempts to prompt the user for input, asking for the first number with input(), but there's a missing closing parenthesis after the input() function call. To fix this, add the closing parenthesis at the end of input("Enter first number: "). Similarly, there's another missing parenthesis in the line where the second number is being input. You need to add that closing parenthesis as well.

Finally, the program prints the result of adding the two numbers, which is correctly formatted, but once the syntax errors are fixed, the program will work as intended and display the sum of the two numbers.

2.8 Project: A Simple Calculator

Let's combine what you've learned to build a basic calculator.

First, define four functions for the operations:

- The add function takes two arguments, a and b, and returns their sum.
- The subtract function takes two arguments, a and b, and returns the result of subtracting b from a.
- The multiply function takes two arguments, a and b, and returns the product of a and b.
- The divide function takes two arguments, a and b, and returns the result of dividing a by b, but first checks if b is not zero to avoid division by zero. If b is zero, it returns an error message instead.

Then, display the options for the user by printing "Simple Calculator" followed by a list of operations:

1. Add
2. Subtract
3. Multiply
4. Divide

Prompt the user to choose an operation by entering a number, and then ask for the two numbers to perform the calculation. Depending on the user's choice, use a series of if-elif statements to call the appropriate function. If the user selects addition, call the add function and print the result. If they select subtraction, call the subtract function and print the result, and so on for multiplication and division. If the user selects an invalid operation, print "Invalid choice!"

Variables, Data Types, and Basic Syntax: Hands-On with Python

Understanding variables, data types, and basic syntax is crucial when starting your Python journey. These foundational concepts allow you to write programs that manipulate and store information effectively. In this section, we'll cover these topics in an interactive, hands-on way that goes beyond theory, ensuring you not only learn but also apply these concepts immediately.

1. Variables: Storing Data with Ease

A **variable** is a container for storing data. You can think of it like a labeled box where you can place information and retrieve it whenever you need it.

The **syntax** for creating a variable is simple: you assign a **value** to a **variable name** using the equal sign (=). For example, you might write variable_name = value.

When naming variables, it's important to follow certain rules:

- A variable name must start with a letter or an underscore.
- It cannot contain spaces or special characters.
- Variable names are case-sensitive, meaning that Name and name would be considered two different variables.

For example, you can create a variable called age and assign it the value 25, or create a variable name and assign it the value "Alice". If you have a variable is_student set to True, you can then use these variables in expressions. For instance, printing f"{name} is {age} years old." will output "Alice is 25 years old.".

Hands-On Exercise:

Here's how you can write a program that asks for a user's name and age, then prints a personalized message using the information entered.

First, prompt the user to **enter their name** by using the input() function. Store the name in a variable called name. Then, ask the user to **enter their age**. Since the age is a number, use the int() function to convert the input into an integer and store it in a variable called age.

Finally, use a **print statement** with an **f-string** to display a message. The message will greet the user by their name and tell them how old they are. For example, the message could read, "Hello, [name]! You are [age] years old." This will dynamically display the user's name and age based on their input.

Challenge: Extend the program to calculate the year the user will turn 100.

2. Data Types: The Building Blocks of Information

Python has various **data types** to handle different kinds of information. The most common data types include:

1. **Integer (int)**, which represents whole numbers.
2. **Float (float)**, which represents numbers with decimals.
3. **String (str)**, which represents text.
4. **Boolean (bool)**, which represents True or False values.
5. **NoneType**, which represents the absence of a value.

In this interactive example, you can check the type of a variable by using the type() function:

- If you have a variable named age set to 30, you can check its type by calling print(type(age)). This will output <class 'int'>, indicating that the variable is an integer.
- If you set a variable price to 19.99, and then check the type by calling print(type(price)), the output will be <class 'float'>, showing that it is a floating-point number.
- If you have a variable greeting set to "Hello, World!", checking the type with print(type(greeting)) will output <class 'str'>, indicating that it's a string.
- If you set a variable is_logged_in to False, checking its type with print(type(is_logged_in)) will return <class 'bool'>, showing that it is a boolean.

For the hands-on exercise, write a program that:

1. Takes the user's **height** and **weight** as input.
2. Calculates their **BMI** using the formula: BMI equals weight in kilograms divided by height in meters squared.
3. Finally, the program prints the user's BMI.

In code, this would involve asking the user for their height and weight, converting the inputs into floats, calculating the BMI, and displaying the result with two decimal places. The output would be formatted like this: print(f"Your BMI is {bmi:.2f}.").

Challenge: Categorize the BMI (e.g., underweight, normal, overweight).

3. Basic Syntax: Writing Clean and Functional Code

Python's syntax is simple and intuitive, designed to be beginner-friendly while remaining powerful.

Hands-On Syntax Practice

To calculate the total price of items in a shopping cart, you would start by prompting the user to enter the price of the first item and store it as a float in a variable named item1. Then, you ask for the price of the second item and store that as item2. Afterward, you calculate the total price by adding item1 and item2 together, storing the result in a variable called total. Finally, you print the total price, formatting it to display two decimal places for currency, such as print(f"Total price: ${total:.2f}"). This will show the total price in a user-friendly format.**Challenge**: Add a 10% discount for totals above $50.

4. Combining Variables, Data Types, and Syntax

Now that we've covered the basics, let's combine these concepts into a mini-project.

Mini-Project: A Simple Interest Calculator

Create a program that calculates the simple interest based on the formula:

To calculate the interest on a loan, you would first prompt the user to enter the principal amount, which is the initial sum of money. You store this value as a float in a variable called principal. Then, you ask the user for the annual interest rate in percentage, storing it in a variable called rate.

You also ask for the time period in years, storing this value as time.

The interest is calculated using the formula: Interest equals Principal multiplied by Rate, multiplied by Time, all divided by 100. This formula is implemented by multiplying the values of principal, rate, and time, and then dividing the result by 100.

Finally, the program outputs the calculated interest, showing the result to the user.print(f"The simple interest is: ${interest:.2f}")

Challenge: Modify the program to calculate compound interest.

5. Debugging and Error Handling

No learning experience is complete without encountering errors! Python provides helpful error messages to guide you in fixing problems.

Common Errors:

A **SyntaxError** occurs when the code is not formatted correctly. For example, if you try to print "Hello World" but forget to close the parentheses like this: print("Hello World", the code will throw a **SyntaxError** because the parentheses are not properly matched.

A **TypeError** happens when incompatible data types are used together. For instance, if you try to concatenate a string with an integer like this: print("Age: " + 25), it will result in a **TypeError** because you can't directly add a string and an integer without converting the integer to a string first.

Quick Fix Tips for Common Beginner Mistakes

Learning Python is exciting, but like any new skill, beginners often encounter common mistakes that can lead to frustration. This section highlights these pitfalls and offers actionable "Quick Fix" tips to help you overcome them easily.

1. Forgetting to Use Indentation

Python uses indentation to define blocks of code, such as those in loops, conditionals, or functions. Missing or inconsistent indentation can cause a IndentationError.

Example Error:

python

```
if True:
print("This will cause an error.")
```

Let's take a look at some common Python mistakes and how to fix them, step by step. Along the way, I'll also share quick tips and solutions that will help you write cleaner, more efficient code.

Mistake 1: Indentation Errors

Python relies heavily on proper indentation. For example, it expects you to use consistent spacing—usually four spaces per indentation level.

A quick fix? Use an integrated development environment, or IDE, like PyCharm or Visual Studio Code. These tools automatically manage indentation for you. Here's an example of properly indented code:

'If True:
print("This will work correctly.")'

With the correct indentation, Python runs this code without a hitch.

Mistake 2: Using the Wrong Variable Name

Remember, Python is case-sensitive, which means name and Name are treated as completely different variables.

Here's an example of what can go wrong:

'Name = "Alice"
print(name)'

This code will throw a NameError because the variable name doesn't exist—it's a typo!

To fix it, double-check your variable names for correct spelling and capitalization. Here's the corrected version:

'name = "Alice"
print(name)'

Mistake 3: Mixing Data Types

Python raises a TypeError if you try to combine incompatible types, like adding a string to an integer.

Here's an example:
'age = 25
print("Age: " + age)'

This code will fail because you're trying to add a string and an integer.

To fix this, you can convert the integer to a string using the str() function, like this:
'print("Age: " + str(age))'

Or, better yet, use an f-string for cleaner and more readable code:
'print(f"Age: {age}")'

Mistake 4: Forgetting to Close Parentheses or Quotation Marks

Unclosed parentheses or mismatched quotation marks will trigger a SyntaxError.

For example:
'print("Hello, World!)'

Notice the missing closing quote? To fix this, simply make sure every opening parenthesis or quote has a matching closing pair:
'print("Hello, World!")'

Using an IDE with syntax highlighting can make spotting these mistakes a breeze.

Mistake 5: Misusing the input() Function

By default, the input() function returns a string. If you forget to convert it to a number, it can lead to unexpected results.

For instance:
'number = input("Enter a number: ")
print(number * 2)'

This code will repeat the string instead of performing arithmetic. To fix it, convert the input to an integer using the int() function:

```
'number = int(input("Enter a number: "))
print(number * 2)'
```

Mistake 6: Ignoring Python's Zero-Based Indexing

Lists and strings in Python are indexed starting from zero. If you try to access an invalid index, you'll get an IndexError.

Here's an example:
```
'fruits = ["apple", "banana", "cherry"]
print(fruits[3])'
```

This will fail because there's no fourth element in the list. To fix it, remember that the last valid index is len(fruits) - 1. In this case, fruits[2] will give you the last element:
```
'print(fruits[2])'
```

Interactive Quiz: Test Your Knowledge

Let's see how well you've been paying attention.

Question 1: What's wrong with this code?
```
'if True
print("Hello!")'
```

A) Missing parentheses
B) Missing colon
C) Missing indentation
D) No error

Answer: B (The code is missing a colon after if True).

Question 2: What will this code output?
```
'num = 5
print("Number: " + num)'
```

A) Number: 5
B) TypeError

C) Number:
D) None

Answer: B (A TypeError occurs because num is an integer).

Question 3: How can you fix this code?
'my_list = [10, 20, 30]
print(my_list[3])'

A) Replace 3 with 2
B) Add more elements to my_list
C) Use slicing like my_list[:3]
D) All of the above

Answer: D (All of these fixes work).

Checklist for Mastering the Basics

Use this checklist to track your progress as you build your Python skills:

Variables and Data Types

- I can define variables with descriptive names.
- I understand Python's common data types, like integers, floats, strings, and booleans.
- I know how to convert between types using functions like int(), str(), and float().

Basic Syntax

- I write clean, indented code.
- I use comments to document my code.
- I avoid common syntax errors, such as unclosed parentheses or missing colons.

Interactive Input and Output

- I can take user input using the input() function.
- I know how to convert input to the correct data type.
- I can format strings using f-strings or concatenation.

Debugging Skills

- I can read and understand Python error messages.
- I know how to fix common errors like SyntaxError, TypeError, and NameError.

Practical Exercises

- I've completed at least three interactive coding exercises.
- I've debugged at least one piece of faulty code.
- I've created a mini-project that combines variables, data types, and basic syntax.

By following these tips and practicing regularly, you'll build a strong foundation in Python programming."

Chapter 3: The Project Approach: Building Your First Python Application

Welcome to Chapter 3! This is where we bring all the concepts you've learned so far to life by building your very first Python application. Think of this as moving from theory to practice — a crucial step in your journey to mastering Python. By the end of this chapter, you'll not only have a working application but also the confidence to tackle new projects on your own.

Why Take the Project Approach?

Before diving in, let's take a moment to understand why the project approach is so effective. When you build an application, you're not just writing code — you're solving a real problem. This hands-on process helps you connect abstract concepts, like variables and loops, to tangible results. Plus, there's no better feeling than seeing your code actually *do something*.

Think of it like learning to cook. Reading recipes is helpful, but it's not until you've prepared a meal that you truly understand how the ingredients work together. Similarly, building a Python project helps you integrate the ingredients of coding — syntax, logic, and problem-solving — into a meaningful whole.

Getting Started: The Planning Phase

Every great project starts with a plan. Let's take a few moments to outline the application we'll build together. For this chapter, we'll create a **simple calculator**. Why a calculator? Because it's practical, easy to understand, and covers core programming concepts like:

- Taking user input
- Performing calculations
- Handling errors gracefully
- Displaying results

Step 1: Define the Purpose

The purpose of our calculator is simple: It will allow users to add, subtract, multiply, and divide numbers. Along the way, you'll learn how to:

1. Use the input() function to gather information.
2. Perform arithmetic operations with Python.
3. Manage errors, such as dividing by zero, using exception handling.

Step 2: Outline the Features

Here's what our calculator will do:

- Ask the user to input two numbers.
- Prompt the user to select an operation: addition, subtraction, multiplication, or division.
- Perform the chosen operation and display the result.
- Handle invalid inputs gracefully by giving the user helpful feedback.

Step 3: Writing the Code

Now, it's time to write some code! As we go through each step, I'll narrate the process so you can follow along and understand what's happening.

Part 1: Setting Up the Basics

First, we'll start by gathering user input. Let's write a Python program that asks the user for two numbers.

Here's the code:

python

Copy code

```python
# Ask the user for two numbers

num1 = float(input("Enter the first number: "))

num2 = float(input("Enter the second number: "))
```

What's happening here? The input() function collects data from the user as a string, but we use float() to convert that data into numbers. This way, our calculator can handle decimals like 2.5 and 3.7.

Part 2: Choosing an Operation

Next, we'll let the user select an operation.

python

Copy code

```python
# Display the operation menu
```

```python
print("Select an operation:")

print("1. Addition")

print("2. Subtraction")

print("3. Multiplication")

print("4. Division")


# Get the user's choice

operation = input("Enter the number corresponding to your choice: ")
```

Here, we provide a menu so users can see their options. Notice that the operation variable stores their choice as a string.

Part 3: Performing the Calculation

Now, we'll use conditional statements to determine which operation the user selected.

python

Copy code

```python
# Perform the chosen operation

if operation == "1":

    result = num1 + num2
```

```python
        print(f"The result of addition is: {result}")

elif operation == "2":

    result = num1 - num2

    print(f"The result of subtraction is: {result}")

elif operation == "3":

    result = num1 * num2

    print(f"The result of multiplication is: {result}")

elif operation == "4":

    if num2 != 0:

        result = num1 / num2

        print(f"The result of division is: {result}")

    else:

        print("Error: Division by zero is not allowed.")

else:

    print("Invalid choice. Please restart the program.")
```

Let's break this down:

- We use if-elif statements to check which operation the user chose.

- If the user chooses division, we add an extra check to ensure the second number isn't zero. This prevents a common error in Python.

Part 4: Enhancing User Experience

Let's add a friendly message at the end so the program feels complete.

python

Copy code

```python
print("Thank you for using the calculator. Goodbye!")
```

This simple touch makes the application feel polished and user-friendly.

Running and Testing Your Program

With our code complete, it's time to run and test it. When you run the program, try the following scenarios:

1. Add two numbers, like 5 and 3.
2. Subtract, multiply, and divide numbers.
3. Test what happens if you divide by zero.
4. Enter invalid input, like letters instead of numbers, and observe the program's response.

Reflecting on What You've Learned

Congratulations! You've just built your first Python application. Along the way, you practiced:

- Working with user input

- Using conditional statements
- Handling errors
- Printing results with f-strings

Challenges to Take It Further

Want to take your calculator to the next level? Here are some challenges for you:

1. Add more operations, like exponentiation or modulus.
2. Allow the user to perform multiple calculations without restarting the program.
3. Add input validation to ensure the user enters numbers instead of text.

Each of these enhancements will deepen your understanding of Python and make your calculator even more powerful.

Summary and Next Steps

In this chapter, you transformed concepts into a working application. By taking the project approach, you gained practical experience in planning, coding, and testing. As you continue your Python journey, remember that building projects is one of the best ways to learn.

In the next chapter, we'll dive into **functions** — a powerful tool for organizing and reusing your code. Until then, keep coding and experimenting. You're doing amazing work!

Chapter 4: Mastering Problem-Solving with Python

Problem-solving is at the heart of programming. Python's simplicity and versatility make it an excellent tool for tackling real-world challenges. In this chapter, we'll explore strategies and techniques to master problem-solving with Python, from understanding problem statements to implementing efficient solutions. By the end of this chapter, you'll be equipped to approach problems with confidence and write clean, effective code.

4.1 Understanding the Problem

Before you start coding, it's crucial to understand the problem fully. Misinterpreting the requirements often leads to incorrect solutions.

Steps to Understand the Problem:

1. **Clarify the Objective**:
   - What is the desired outcome?
   - What input is required, and what output is expected?
2. **Break Down the Problem**:
   - Divide the problem into smaller, manageable parts.
   - Identify constraints and edge cases.
3. **Write a Plan**:
   - Create a step-by-step outline of the solution.
   - Use pseudocode to organize your thoughts.

Example: Find the Largest Number in a List

- **Problem Statement**: Write a program to find the largest number in a list of integers.
- **Input**: A list of integers (e.g., [4, 7, 1, 9, 2]).
- **Output**: The largest integer (e.g., 9).

4.2 Algorithm Design

An algorithm is a step-by-step procedure for solving a problem. Good algorithms are efficient and easy to understand.

Designing the Algorithm:

1. Initialize a variable to store the largest number (max_num).
2. Loop through the list, comparing each element with max_num.
3. Update max_num if a larger number is found.

4.3 Breaking Down Real-World Problems

Let's apply problem-solving techniques to common scenarios.

Problem 1: FizzBuzz

Write a program that prints numbers from 1 to 100. For multiples of 3, print "Fizz"; for multiples of 5, print "Buzz"; for multiples of both, print "FizzBuzz."

Steps to Solve:

1. Loop through numbers 1 to 100.

2. Check divisibility by 3 and 5 using the modulus operator (%).
3. Print the appropriate output.

Problem 2: Palindrome Checker

Write a program to check if a string is a palindrome (reads the same backward as forward).

Steps to Solve:

1. Remove spaces and convert the string to lowercase.
2. Compare the string with its reverse.

Problem 3: Finding the Missing Number

Given a list of integers from 1 to n with one missing number, find the missing number.

Steps to Solve:

1. Calculate the sum of numbers from 1 to n using the formula: $\text{Sum} = \frac{n \times (n + 1)}{2}$
2. Subtract the sum of the given list from the calculated sum.

4.4 Optimizing Solutions

Efficiency matters in programming, especially when dealing with large datasets or complex computations.

Common Optimization Techniques:

1. **Avoid Nested Loops**: Use single loops or mathematical formulas.
2. **Leverage Python Libraries**: Libraries like NumPy and Pandas are optimized for performance.
3. **Use Built-In Functions**: Python's built-in functions (e.g., max(), sum()) are faster than manually iterating through lists.

Debugging Tips:

1. **Read Error Messages**: Understand what the error means.
2. **Print Statements**: Use print() to trace variables and logic.
3. **Use Debugging Tools**: Tools like PyCharm's debugger allow you to step through code.

Example: Debugging a Missing Number Program:

If the code gives incorrect output:

python

```python
nums = [1, 2, 3, 5]
n = 5
print(sum(nums))  # Debug by checking intermediate calculations
```

4.6 Practice Problems

Solve these problems to reinforce your problem-solving skills:

1. Write a program to reverse the words in a sentence.
2. Create a function that calculates the factorial of a number.
3. Find the second-largest number in a list.

Mastering Programming Logic and Algorithms with Real-World Python Applications

Programming logic and algorithms form the backbone of problem-solving in software development. Logic provides a structured way to think about problems, while algorithms define step-by-step solutions. Python's simplicity and rich ecosystem make it ideal for implementing these concepts, enabling developers to solve complex problems in various domains.

This chapter will discuss essential programming logic and algorithms, along with real-world scenarios where Python shines in solving intricate challenges.

1. Essential Programming Logic

Programming logic involves creating a flow of actions that lead to the desired outcome. This requires an understanding of control structures, data organization, and iterative processes.

1.1 Control Structures

Control structures dictate the flow of a program. Python offers several tools to implement logical decisions and loops.

1. **Conditional Statements**:
   - Use if, elif, and else to make decisions.

2. **Loops**:
    - Use for and while loops for repetitive tasks.
3. **Nested Logic**:
    - Combine loops and conditions for complex workflows.

1.2 Algorithms

An algorithm is a step-by-step procedure to solve a problem. Common algorithms include:

1. **Sorting**:
    - Algorithms like Bubble Sort, Merge Sort, and Quick Sort arrange data in a specified order.
2. **Searching**:
    - Algorithms like Binary Search efficiently locate elements in sorted data.

In this section, we'll dive into how a **binary search** algorithm works, which is an efficient method for searching for a specific element in a **sorted list**.

Imagine you have a list of numbers sorted in ascending order, like [1, 3, 5, 7, 9], and you want to find the number 7. Instead of checking each element one by one, binary search works by repeatedly dividing the list in half and comparing the target number with the middle element.

Here's the process in simpler terms:

First, you start with two pointers: one at the beginning of the list (the "left" pointer) and one at the end (the "right" pointer). The key idea is to focus on the middle of the list. If the middle element is the one you're looking for, you've found your answer and can stop right there.

If the middle element isn't the target, then the search continues either to the left or the right half of the list. If the target number is greater than the middle element, you discard the left half of the list and search the right half. Conversely, if the target is smaller, you discard the right half and continue searching in the left half.

This process is repeated until either you find the target or the search interval becomes empty, meaning the target isn't in the list.

In the example given, when searching for the number 7, the algorithm will quickly hone in on the correct position by reducing the range of numbers to check. This is much faster than checking each element individually, especially for large lists.

Binary search works best when the list is already sorted. Its efficiency comes from the fact that each comparison reduces the search space by half, making it much quicker than linear search for large datasets.

3. **Recursion**:
   - A function calls itself to solve smaller instances of a problem.

In this example, we're going to explore how to calculate the **factorial** of a number using recursion.

A **factorial** of a number is the product of all positive integers less than or equal to that number. For example, the factorial of 5, written as 5!, is:

5! = 5 × 4 × 3 × 2 × 1 = 120.

The function we use to calculate the factorial is **recursive**, meaning it calls itself to break down the problem into smaller and simpler parts.

Here's how it works:

1. The function factorial checks if the number is either 0 or 1. This is the **base case**, and in these cases, the factorial is defined as 1. This is because 0! and 1! are both equal to 1 by definition.
2. If the number is greater than 1, the function calls itself with the number reduced by 1, multiplying the result by the current number. This continues until the base case (0 or 1) is reached.

For example, if you call factorial(5), the function will calculate:

5 × factorial(4) → 5 × (4 × factorial(3)) → 5 × 4 × (3 × factorial(2)) → 5 × 4 × 3 × (2 × factorial(1)) → 5 × 4 × 3 × 2 × 1 = 120.

This approach breaks down the larger problem into smaller steps, each one easier to solve, until the solution is built up from the base case.

In the example provided, factorial(5) will return **120**, which is the correct result for 5!.

2. Real-World Scenarios Where Python Solves Complex Problems

Python is widely used to address intricate challenges across various industries. Here are real-world scenarios showcasing its problem-solving power.

2.1 Data Analysis and Visualization

Python simplifies data analysis with libraries like Pandas and Matplotlib.

Scenario: Analyze sales data to identify trends.

In this example, we'll explore how to **visualize data** using a simple **line plot** to display sales trends across different months.

First, we start by importing the necessary libraries. We use **pandas** to handle and organize the data in a table format, and **matplotlib.pyplot** to create the plot.

We then define the data. Here, we create a dictionary containing two keys: Month and Sales. The Month key holds a list of months, while the Sales key holds the sales values for each corresponding month. We use **pandas' DataFrame** to convert this dictionary into a structured table.

After preparing the data, we create the plot with the plt.plot() function. We plot the months on the x-axis and the sales on the y-axis, with a marker at each data point for better visibility. We also set the title of the graph to "Monthly Sales" and label the axes for clarity.

Finally, we use plt.show() to display the plot, which will show a line graph of sales trends over the months of January, February, March, and April.

The output will visually represent the fluctuations in sales, making it easier to understand the pattern of sales growth or decline over time.

Impact: Businesses can make data-driven decisions by visualizing performance trends.

2.2 Machine Learning and AI

Python's scikit-learn and TensorFlow libraries power machine learning applications.

Impact: Network administrators can identify vulnerabilities and secure their systems.

3. Tips for Mastering Problem-Solving

1. **Practice Algorithms**:
   - Solve problems on platforms like LeetCode, HackerRank, or Codewars.
2. **Think in Steps**:
   - Write pseudocode before coding.
   - Focus on logic, not syntax.
3. **Debug Methodically**:
   - Use print() statements or a debugger to trace errors.
   - Test your code with edge cases.
4. **Learn from Others**:
   - Review open-source projects to understand different approaches.

Mastering Classic Problems in Python: Step-by-Step Solutions

Classic problems like **FizzBuzz**, **Binary Search**, and **Sorting Algorithms** are cornerstones of programming education. These problems help you understand fundamental concepts, sharpen your logic, and build confidence in solving real-world challenges. This chapter provides detailed, step-by-step solutions to these problems and includes bonus challenges for advanced learners to take their skills to the next level.

1. FizzBuzz: A Simple Introduction to Problem Solving

Write a program that prints numbers from 1 to 100:

- For multiples of 3, print "Fizz".
- For multiples of 5, print "Buzz".
- For multiples of both, print "FizzBuzz".
- Otherwise, print the number.

Step-by-Step Solution

1. **Understand the Problem**:
    - Iterate through numbers from 1 to 100.
    - Use the modulus operator (%) to check divisibility.
2. **Plan the Logic**:
    - Check for multiples of 3 and 5 first (to avoid overlapping conditions).
    - Use elif to handle other cases.

4. **Test the Solution**:

- Verify outputs for numbers like 3, 5, 15, and others to ensure correctness.

Bonus Challenge for Advanced Learners

- **Generate FizzBuzz for Any Range**: Write a function that accepts a range and custom divisors:

2. Binary Search: Efficient Searching

Write a function that uses the binary search algorithm to find a target value in a sorted list. Return the index of the target or -1 if it is not found.

Step-by-Step Solution

- **Understand the Problem**:
    - Binary search works by repeatedly dividing the search interval in half.
    - Only applicable to sorted lists.
- **Plan the Logic**:
    - Define the initial search range (left and right).
    - Calculate the midpoint and compare it with the target value.
    - Narrow the search range based on the comparison.

4. **Test the Solution**:
    - Test with different targets, including edge cases like the smallest and largest numbers in the list.

Bonus Challenge for Advanced Learners

- **Recursive Binary Search**: Implement binary search using recursion:

3. Sorting Algorithms: Organizing Data

Write functions to implement common sorting algorithms, such as Bubble Sort and Quick Sort.

Step-by-Step Solution: Bubble Sort

1. **Understand the Problem**:
   - Bubble Sort repeatedly compares adjacent elements and swaps them if they are in the wrong order.
   - The process continues until the list is sorted.
2. **Plan the Logic**:
   - Use nested loops: the outer loop controls passes, and the inner loop handles comparisons and swaps.

Test the Solution:

- Verify the output with both sorted and unsorted inputs.

Step-by-Step Solution: Quick Sort

1. **Understand the Problem**:
   - Quick Sort selects a pivot and partitions the list into two sublists: elements smaller than the pivot and elements larger than the pivot.
2. **Plan the Logic**:

- Use recursion to sort sublists.

3. **Code**:

Test the Solution:

- Test with large datasets to observe the efficiency of Quick Sort.

Bonus Challenge for Advanced Learners

- **Optimize Quick Sort**: Implement Quick Sort with a randomized pivot for better performance on already sorted inputs.
- **Compare Sorting Algorithms**: Write a program to compare the execution time of Bubble Sort and Quick Sort on the same dataset:

Chapter 5: Intermediate Python: Unlocking Advanced Concepts

Once you've mastered Python basics, the next step is to delve into intermediate concepts that unlock the language's full potential. This chapter introduces advanced Python features such as object-oriented programming (OOP), file handling, decorators, and working with modules and libraries. These concepts are essential for building robust, scalable, and efficient Python applications.

5.1 Object-Oriented Programming (OOP)

Object-oriented programming is a paradigm that organizes code into reusable objects that encapsulate data and behavior.

Key Concepts of Object-Oriented Programming (OOP) in Python

1. **Classes and Objects**
   In Python, a **class** serves as a blueprint for creating objects. Think of it as a template that defines the properties and behaviors that objects will have. An **object** is an instance of a class, and each object can hold different values for its properties.

   For example, imagine a class named Dog. It could define attributes like the dog's name and breed, and it might also include behaviors, such as a bark method. You can create individual dog objects from this class, each with its own name and breed.

2. **Inheritance**
   Inheritance allows one class to inherit the attributes

and methods of another class. This is useful when you want to create a new class that shares common features with an existing one, but with some specific differences.

For instance, you could have a general class called Animal, which has a species attribute. Then, you could create a Dog class that inherits from Animal, adding its own properties, like name and breed. This way, the Dog class can reuse functionality from Animal, avoiding code repetition.

3. **Polymorphism**
   Polymorphism refers to the ability of different classes to have methods with the same name but perform different tasks. This allows you to use the same method name across various classes while ensuring each class's method performs its intended action.

   For example, both a Cat class and a Dog class could have a method named sound, but the Cat would return "Meow!" and the Dog would return "Woof!" Despite having the same method name, they behave differently based on the class they're in.

Working with Files in Python

Python provides powerful tools to work with files, making it easy to read, write, and manipulate data stored in files.

1. **Writing to a File**
   To write data to a file, you can use Python's built-in open() function with the "w" mode. This allows you to open a file for writing and add content to it. If the file doesn't exist, Python will create it for you.
2. **Reading from a File**
   If you want to read the contents of a file, you can use

the open() function with the "r" mode. Once the file is opened, you can use methods like read() to access its contents.

3. **Appending to a File**
   To add data to an existing file without overwriting its contents, you can open the file in "a" mode. This appends the new content to the end of the file.

Modules and Libraries in Python

Python has a rich ecosystem of built-in and third-party libraries that save time and effort during development. You can import these modules to add new functionality to your programs.

1. **Built-in Modules**
   Python includes several built-in modules, such as math for mathematical operations and datetime for working with dates and times. You can easily import these modules and start using their functions.

2. **Third-Party Libraries**
   In addition to built-in modules, Python also supports third-party libraries. These libraries can be installed via a package manager called pip. For example, you can install requests to interact with web APIs and fetch data from websites.

Decorators in Python

A **decorator** is a function that allows you to modify or extend the behavior of other functions without changing their code. It's like adding a layer of functionality around a function.

For example, you could use a decorator to log the execution time of a function or to validate its inputs before running it. Decorators are widely used in situations where you need to add reusable functionality to multiple functions.

Generators in Python

A **generator** is a special type of function that allows you to create iterators in a memory-efficient way. Instead of generating all values at once, a generator yields one value at a time, which makes it suitable for working with large datasets.

Using the yield keyword, a generator can pause its execution and return a value. The function can resume from where it left off when requested for the next value.

Error Handling in Python

Python provides error-handling mechanisms to manage unexpected situations. The try and except blocks allow you to catch errors and handle them gracefully, ensuring that your program doesn't crash unexpectedly.

You can also define your own **custom exceptions** to handle specific error scenarios in your program, providing more clarity and control over error handling.

Working with APIs in Python

APIs (Application Programming Interfaces) allow different applications to communicate with each other. Python makes it easy to interact with APIs, allowing your program to fetch data from external services, like a weather API or a financial data provider.

Using libraries like requests, you can send HTTP requests to fetch data, which can then be processed and displayed in your application.

Context Managers in Python

A **context manager** is a tool in Python that helps manage resources, such as files or database connections, by ensuring they are properly opened and closed. Context managers are used with the with statement, which automatically takes care of resource management, even if an error occurs.

For example, when working with files, the with statement ensures the file is closed properly after you're done working with it, which helps prevent resource leaks.

These concepts are foundational to writing efficient, reusable, and clean code in Python. Understanding them will help you leverage the full potential of Python, making your programs more powerful and maintainable.

Bonus Challenge:

Build a program that fetches weather data from a public API and displays it in a user-friendly format.

Context Managers

Context managers simplify resource management, such as file handling or database connections.

Example:
python

```
with open("example.txt", "r") as file:
    content = file.read()
    print(content)
```

Intermediate Python: Exploring Data Structures and Object-Oriented Programming

Data structures and Object-Oriented Programming (OOP) are foundational concepts for writing efficient and scalable Python applications. Data structures allow us to organize and manipulate data effectively, while OOP provides a blueprint for building reusable and modular code. In this chapter, we'll explore Python's core data structures—lists, dictionaries, and sets—with visual aids to simplify learning, followed by an introduction to OOP using relatable analogies to clarify its principles.

1. Data Structures in Python
1.1 Lists

A **list** is an ordered collection of items, which can be of any data type. Lists are dynamic, meaning you can add, remove, or modify elements.

1. Visualizing Lists

Imagine you have a row of labeled containers, each holding an item. The first container might hold a number, the second one a piece of fruit, the third might have a decimal, and the last container could hold a true/false value. Each of these containers represents an element in a list.

For example, think of a list of fruits. You could have "Apple", "Banana", and "Cherry" in a row. Each item has a position or "index" that tells you where it is in the list. If you want to access an item, you simply refer to its position.

You can also add new items to the list or remove them. For instance, you could add "Orange" at the end or insert "Grape" in a specific position. Similarly, you can remove an item by its name or position, or even loop through the list to see each item one by one.

A common use for lists might be managing a to-do list in an app—adding tasks, removing completed ones, or viewing your tasks in order.

2. Dictionaries

Think of a dictionary like a real-world dictionary, where a word (the key) maps to its definition (the value). In programming, a dictionary stores data in key-value pairs. So instead of just having a list of items, you can have a "word" that points to its "meaning".

For example, you might have a dictionary where "Name" maps to "Alice", "Age" maps to 25, and "Country" maps to "USA". To get the value associated with a key, you simply refer to that key. You can also add new key-value pairs, update existing ones, or remove them. If you need to go through all the items in a dictionary, you can loop over the keys and values to get the full picture.

Dictionaries are really useful when you're managing user data, like storing information for a web application.

3. Sets

A set is like a bag full of unique items, where no duplicates are allowed. So if you add the same item twice, it will only appear once in the set. Sets are great when you need to find common items, or differences, between two groups.

For example, imagine you have a set of numbers, and you want to see if a particular number is in the set. You can also combine two sets, find items that appear in both, or even figure out what's different between the sets.

A practical use for sets might be tracking unique visitors to a website, ensuring no one is counted more than once.

Object-Oriented Programming (OOP)

What is OOP?

Object-Oriented Programming is a way of organizing code around objects, which are real-world things represented in your program. Each object has two things: attributes (the properties) and behaviors (the things it can do).

For example, think of a car. The car has attributes like its color, make, and model. It also has behaviors, like being able to start, stop, or accelerate. In OOP, a car would be a *class*, and a specific car (say, a red Toyota Corolla) would be an *instance* of that class.

Defining a Class

A class is like a blueprint. It defines the general properties and behaviors, but doesn't create a specific car. To do that, you "instantiate" the class, creating an object, like your Toyota Corolla.

Key Concepts in OOP

1. **Encapsulation**: This is about bundling data and behaviors into a single unit. For example, all the details about the car (like make and model) are inside the car object, and you interact with those details through defined methods like "start".
2. **Inheritance**: This allows a new class to inherit properties and behaviors from an existing one. For example, you might create an ElectricCar class that inherits from the regular Car class, and then adds its own unique behavior, like the ability to charge.

3. **Polymorphism**: This is about having different classes share the same method name but behave differently. So, you could have a method called "start" in both a regular car and an electric car, but each one would do something different when you call it.
4. **Abstraction**: This is hiding the complex details and exposing only what's necessary. For example, when you drive a car, you don't need to know how the engine works—just how to start the car and drive it.

OOP in Action: Banking System

In OOP, you could model a banking system with a BankAccount class. The BankAccount class would define properties like the account holder's name and balance, and behaviors like deposit and withdraw. You could then create instances of BankAccount for different users and interact with their accounts by calling the methods defined in the class.

Avoiding Mistakes and Future-Proofing Your Code

Object-Oriented Programming is a powerful tool, but there are some common mistakes to avoid:

1. **Ignoring Encapsulation**: If you let others change an object's internal state directly, it could lead to errors. Instead, you should control how others can access or change the object's properties.
2. **Overcomplicating with Too Many Classes**: Creating too many classes for every little thing can make your code messy. Try to keep things simple and use inheritance to share common behaviors.
3. **Overusing Inheritance**: While inheritance is useful, it can lead to complicated code if overused. Sometimes, composition (putting objects together instead of inheriting from them) is a better solution.

4. **Forgetting Polymorphism**: Polymorphism allows you to simplify your code by having similar methods in different classes. Without it, you might end up repeating yourself unnecessarily.
5. **Neglecting Documentation**: If you don't document your code, it can be difficult for others (or even yourself) to understand it later. Always add comments and explanations where needed.

By following these practices, OOP helps you build scalable, flexible, and maintainable code that can grow and adapt over time. Whether you're designing a simple app or a large system, these principles ensure your code is both efficient and easy to manage.

Chapter 6: Python in Action: Real-World Projects

Learning Python becomes truly rewarding when you apply its concepts to solve real-world problems. In this chapter, we'll dive into real-world projects that demonstrate Python's power and versatility. These projects cover areas like data analysis, automation, web development, and machine learning, showcasing practical implementations of Python in various industries. By the end of this chapter, you'll have a deeper understanding of how Python can be used to create impactful solutions.

Project 1: Automating File Organization

The problem at hand is a familiar one: manually sorting through files on a computer is tedious and time-consuming. Imagine a cluttered folder with hundreds of files, and you need to organize them based on their type—documents, images, videos, etc. A Python script can easily automate this process.

Step 1: Setting Up

First, you'll need to define the directory where your files are located. The goal is to organize files by their extensions— like moving all .txt files into a "Documents" folder, .jpg files into an "Images" folder, and so on.

Step 2: The Python Script

Using Python's built-in os and shutil modules, this script will automatically create folders for different file types and move the files into their corresponding folders. It saves you hours of manual work.

Result:

By running this script, your files are automatically sorted into their appropriate categories, keeping your folders neat and organized.

Project 2: Data Analysis with Pandas

Let's say you have a dataset, maybe related to sales or some other business activity, and you need to extract insights like total revenue, average sales, or even the best-performing product. This can easily be achieved using Python's Pandas library.

Step 1: Loading the Data

We begin by loading a CSV file containing sales data. The pandas library makes this easy by converting the dataset into a format we can manipulate.

Step 2: Analyzing the Data

Next, we calculate the total revenue, average sales, and identify which product performed the best. Pandas makes these calculations straightforward, turning raw data into meaningful insights.

Result:

The analysis helps make data-driven decisions, such as understanding trends and spotting opportunities for growth.

Project 3: Web Scraping with BeautifulSoup

Web scraping is the process of extracting data from websites. This project focuses on scraping job postings from a website and saving them in a CSV file for easy analysis.

Step 1: Installing Libraries

To scrape data, you'll need to install the requests library to fetch the webpage and BeautifulSoup to parse the HTML content.

Step 2: The Script

Once you have the page content, the script will find job postings, extract relevant details (like job titles, companies, and locations), and save them in a CSV file.

Result:

The output is a CSV file with structured job data, which can be further analyzed or used to apply for jobs.

Project 4: Building a Simple Flask Web App

Have you ever wanted to build a web app that collects and displays user feedback? Flask is a great framework for building simple web applications, and in this project, you'll create an app where users can submit feedback and see what others have said.

Step 1: Setting Up Flask

Flask is a micro-framework for Python that makes it easy to get a web app up and running quickly. We install it and set up a basic app to handle form submissions.

Step 2: The App

The app will have two pages: one for submitting feedback and one for displaying all the feedback collected. It's a basic app, but a great start for anyone interested in web development.

Result:

You'll have a functional web app that users can interact with—simple, yet powerful.

Project 5: Predicting House Prices with Machine Learning

Predicting house prices is a common machine learning task. In this project, you'll train a model to predict house prices based on features like size and the number of rooms.

Step 1: Setting Up the Model

We begin by installing the necessary libraries—scikit-learn for machine learning and pandas for data manipulation. Then we load a dataset containing features about houses.

Step 2: Training the Model

Using a linear regression model, the script will learn from the dataset and be able to predict the price of a house based on its size and number of rooms.

Result:

This machine learning model can be used by real estate professionals to estimate house prices more effectively.

Practical Projects: Web Scraper, Chatbot, and Finance Tracker

The following projects are designed to deepen your Python skills by building real-world applications:

1. **Web Scraper to Gather Data from Websites**

- This project will help you automate the extraction of data, like job postings or news articles, and save it in a CSV file for later use.
- You'll use the requests library to fetch web pages and BeautifulSoup to extract the data you need.

2. **Basic Chatbot Using Python Libraries**
   - A chatbot is a great way to learn how to use Natural Language Processing (NLP). This project uses Python's nltk library to create a simple rule-based chatbot that responds to user input.

3. **Personal Finance Tracker with Data Visualization**
   - Track your income and expenses with a personal finance tracker that uses pandas to store data and matplotlib to visualize it. You can see your spending habits at a glance and make informed financial decisions.

Downloadable Templates

In this section, templates for each of the projects above will be provided. You can easily customize these templates for your own use, saving time and allowing you to dive deeper into the learning process.

1. **Web Scraper Template**
   - This template fetches data from a website, extracts useful information, and saves it to a CSV file. It's a great starting point for anyone looking to get into web scraping.

Each of these projects introduces fundamental Python concepts that can be applied to real-world tasks, helping you build both your skills and a portfolio of useful tools.

Chapter 7: Automation Made Easy: Python's Role in Everyday Efficiency

Automation is the backbone of modern productivity, allowing repetitive tasks to be performed faster and with fewer errors. Python's simplicity, extensive library support, and versatility make it one of the best tools for automation. In this chapter, we'll explore how Python can simplify everyday tasks such as file management, email handling, data entry, and more. Through practical examples, you'll discover how to leverage Python to boost your efficiency in personal and professional contexts.

Why Use Python for Automation?

Python's role in automation stems from its features:

1. **Ease of Use**: Python's syntax is beginner-friendly, allowing quick adoption.
2. **Extensive Libraries**: Libraries like os, shutil, smtplib, and pandas simplify tasks such as file handling, email automation, and data processing.
3. **Cross-Platform Compatibility**: Python works seamlessly across Windows, macOS, and Linux.
4. **Scalability**: Automation scripts can start small and scale with complexity as needs grow.

Let's explore some practical scenarios where automation can save time and effort, making your workflows much more efficient.

Scenario 1: Organizing Files Automatically

One common problem people face is managing a messy directory filled with hundreds of files. This can be tedious to organize manually. The solution? Automate the process with a Python script that sorts files into different folders based on their type. For instance, images can be moved to an "Images" folder, documents to a "Documents" folder, and videos to a "Videos" folder. This way, your files are neatly categorized and easy to access.

Scenario 2: Automating Email Sending

Sending repetitive emails can quickly become a time-consuming task. Automating email sending with Python's built-in library, smtplib, allows you to send emails automatically. This is ideal for routine communications, saving you the effort of manually drafting and sending each message.

Scenario 3: Automating Web Interactions

Automating repetitive tasks on websites, such as logging into accounts or filling out forms, can be a game changer. Using the selenium library, you can automate these tasks by simulating user interactions with the web. Whether it's filling out a registration form or logging into your favorite site, Selenium makes it all possible with minimal effort.

Scenario 4: Automating Data Entry

Manual data entry into spreadsheets can be tedious and prone to errors. With Python's pandas library, you can automate the process of entering and processing data. This ensures your data is entered accurately and efficiently, without the hassle of typing everything manually.

Scenario 5: Scheduling Tasks Automatically

Running scripts at specific times manually can be a hassle. Instead, automate the scheduling of tasks using Python's schedule library. You can set up your tasks to run at specific times, like every day at 9:00 AM, so you don't have to worry about manually triggering them.

Best Practices for Automation

Here are some tips to help you get started with automation:

1. **Start Simple**: Begin with small, manageable tasks and scale up as you gain confidence.
2. **Use Libraries**: Take full advantage of Python's extensive library ecosystem to simplify your automation tasks.
3. **Handle Errors Gracefully**: Implement error handling (like try-except blocks) to ensure your automation scripts don't fail unexpectedly.
4. **Test Your Scripts**: Before deploying, always test your scripts in a controlled environment to ensure they work as expected.
5. **Secure Sensitive Data**: Store credentials securely using environment variables or encrypted storage.

Advanced Automation Ideas

For those looking to take automation to the next level, consider these advanced ideas:

1. **Automated Report Generation**: Use Python to generate reports in PDF or Excel formats. Libraries like matplotlib and xlsxwriter can help you create visually appealing reports from data.
2. **API Integration**: Automate tasks like retrieving weather updates or stock market prices using APIs and libraries like requests or flask.

3. **Social Media Automation**: Automate social media posting on platforms like Twitter or LinkedIn using libraries like tweepy and linkedin-api.

Selenium and PyAutoGUI: Power Tools for Automation

Python also offers two incredibly powerful libraries— **Selenium** and **PyAutoGUI**—that can simplify even the most complex workflows.

Selenium is perfect for automating web browsers. Whether it's filling out forms, clicking buttons, or navigating between pages, Selenium can replicate almost any human web interaction. With its ability to automate browsers like Chrome, Firefox, and Edge, it's ideal for web testing, form submissions, and data scraping.

PyAutoGUI excels at automating desktop applications. It lets you simulate mouse movements, click buttons, type on the keyboard, and even take screenshots. It's perfect for automating repetitive tasks in applications like Notepad or Word.

Combining Selenium and PyAutoGUI

If you need to automate both web and desktop tasks, you can combine Selenium and PyAutoGUI for maximum efficiency. For example, you might use Selenium to download a file from a website and then use PyAutoGUI to rename that file on your desktop.

Best Practices for Web and GUI Automation

1. **Use Explicit Waits in Selenium**: To ensure your scripts wait for elements to load properly before interacting with them, use explicit waits in Selenium.

2. **Optimize Image Recognition in PyAutoGUI**: When automating GUI tasks, ensure your images are high resolution for better recognition accuracy.
3. **Test Thoroughly**: Always test your automation scripts in a controlled environment before using them in a live setting.

Automating Repetitive Tasks with Python

Whether it's renaming files, sending emails, or scheduling tasks, Python makes it easy to automate these everyday activities. By learning and applying these tools, you'll be able to boost productivity and reduce the manual effort needed to complete routine tasks.

Chapter 8: Cracking the Code of Data Analysis

Data analysis is a cornerstone of modern decision-making, driving insights in fields like business, healthcare, finance, and technology. Python's data analysis ecosystem, powered by libraries like **Pandas**, **NumPy**, and **Matplotlib**, has made it a go-to language for processing, analyzing, and visualizing data. In this chapter, we'll explore the fundamental steps of data analysis, provide real-world examples, and empower you to uncover actionable insights from raw datasets.

Understanding the Data Analysis Workflow

Effective data analysis involves a structured approach that ensures reliability and accuracy. The key stages include:

1. **Data Collection**:
    - Gather data from sources such as files (CSV, Excel), databases, or APIs.
    - Tools: pandas, sqlite3, requests.
2. **Data Cleaning**:
    - Handle missing values, duplicates, and inconsistencies.
    - Tools: pandas.
3. **Data Exploration**:
    - Summarize and visualize data to identify patterns.
    - Tools: pandas, matplotlib, seaborn.
4. **Data Analysis**:
    - Apply statistical methods or algorithms to derive insights.
    - Tools: numpy, scipy.

5. **Data Visualization**:
    - Present findings through clear and impactful charts.
    - Tools: matplotlib, seaborn.
6. **Report Generation**:
    - Communicate insights through reports or dashboards.
    - Tools: pandas, openpyxl, plotly.

Essential Python Libraries for Data Analysis

1. **Pandas**: Data manipulation and analysis.
    - DataFrames, Series, and data cleaning.
2. **NumPy**: Numerical computations.
    - Multi-dimensional arrays and mathematical functions.
3. **Matplotlib**: Data visualization.
    - Line, bar, scatter, and pie charts.
4. **Seaborn**: Statistical data visualization.
    - Heatmaps, pair plots, and distribution plots.

Practical Examples

Example 1: Analyzing Sales Data

In this example, we'll analyze a retail store's sales data to find the total revenue, best-selling products, and sales trends.

Step 1: Load the Dataset
We begin by loading the sales data into a DataFrame. This lets us explore the data and understand its structure.

Step 2: Data Cleaning
We check for missing values and clean the dataset by removing any incomplete rows.

Step 3: Calculate Total Revenue
Next, we calculate the total revenue by multiplying the quantity sold by the price of each product and then summing up the total revenue.

Step 4: Identify Best-Selling Products
We group the data by product and sum the quantities sold to determine which products are the best sellers.

Step 5: Visualize Sales Trends
Using a line chart, we plot the sales trends over time to observe any patterns or fluctuations in revenue.

Example 2: Cleaning and Analyzing Employee Data

In this example, we'll focus on analyzing employee performance by reviewing their performance scores and identifying trends.

Step 1: Load Data
We load the employee data into a DataFrame to inspect the records.

Step 2: Data Cleaning
We remove duplicates and handle missing performance scores by filling them with the average score.

Step 3: Analyze Performance
We group the data by department and calculate the average performance score for each department to see how different teams are performing.

Step 4: Visualize Performance Distribution
We use a histogram to visualize the distribution of performance scores across employees.

Advanced Data Analysis Techniques

- **Correlation Analysis:**
  We identify relationships between different variables, such as product prices and quantities sold, using a correlation matrix.
- **Pivot Tables:**
  Pivot tables allow us to summarize data dynamically, helping us look at things like total revenue by product and date.
- **Time Series Analysis:**
  By analyzing sales data over time, we can detect patterns such as seasonality or trends, helping forecast future performance.

Challenge of the Week: Analyzing Weather Data

In this challenge, your task is to analyze weather data to determine average temperatures, identify weather patterns, and predict rainfall likelihood.

Goal:

- Calculate average temperatures per month.
- Identify extreme weather days.
- Visualize rainfall patterns.

Mastering Python Libraries for Data Analysis

Python's data analysis capabilities are built on three key libraries: Pandas, NumPy, and Matplotlib. Together, they allow us to clean, analyze, and visualize data efficiently.

1. Pandas: Data Manipulation

Pandas is the most powerful tool for handling structured data. It allows you to clean, filter, group, and analyze data with ease.

Key Features:

- Load data from various file types (CSV, Excel, etc.).
- Handle missing values and duplicates.
- Perform data grouping, aggregation, and more.

2. NumPy: Numerical Computing

NumPy is essential for high-performance numerical calculations. It supports multidimensional arrays and provides various mathematical functions.

Key Features:

- Perform mathematical operations on arrays.
- Generate random numbers and perform statistical calculations.

3. Matplotlib: Data Visualization

Matplotlib helps create static, animated, and interactive plots. It allows you to customize every aspect of your plots.

Key Features:

- Create various types of charts, like line, bar, and scatter plots.
- Customize plots with colors, markers, and labels.

Combining Pandas, NumPy, and Matplotlib: A Complete Data Analysis Workflow

In this section, we walk through the process of cleaning, analyzing, and visualizing sales data using these three libraries. We start by loading and cleaning the data, then calculate insights like monthly sales and product statistics, and finish by visualizing the results with a line plot.

Best Practices for Data Analysis

- Use **Pandas** for handling tabular data and **NumPy** for mathematical operations.
- Optimize performance by leveraging vectorized operations in **NumPy**.
- Keep visualizations simple and clear, focusing on key insights.

Step-by-Step Guide to Cleaning, Analyzing, and Visualizing Data

Data analysis is a process that begins with cleaning and ends with visualizing insights. Here's a step-by-step guide using Python libraries:

Step 1: Data Cleaning

- **Load the Dataset:** Load your data into a Pandas DataFrame.
- **Identify Missing Values:** Check for missing values in your data and handle them by filling in or dropping rows.
- **Remove Duplicates:** Clean up duplicate entries to ensure accuracy.
- **Standardize Data:** Ensure consistency in formats (e.g., dates).

Step 2: Data Analysis

- **Add New Columns:** Create new columns for derived values like revenue.
- **Summarize Data:** Use summary statistics to get an overview of your data.
- **Group and Aggregate:** Group data by categories (e.g., products, months) and perform aggregate functions like sum and average.

Step 3: Data Visualization

- Visualize trends and patterns using line charts, bar charts, and other plot types, making it easier to communicate insights.

Conclusion

In this chapter, we've explored how to effectively clean, analyze, and visualize data using Python's powerful libraries: **Pandas**, **NumPy**, and **Matplotlib**. We began by understanding how to handle and manipulate data, focusing on essential tasks such as data cleaning, identifying missing values, removing duplicates, and standardizing formats. From there, we moved on to the analysis stage, where we calculated key metrics, summarized data, and identified trends using groupings and aggregations.

We then turned to visualizing our results. We saw how Matplotlib enables us to create meaningful charts that help communicate our insights clearly. By applying these techniques, you now have a solid foundation for transforming raw data into actionable insights.

Key Takeaways:

- **Pandas** allows you to manipulate and clean your data effortlessly.
- **NumPy** provides the numerical power to perform advanced calculations.
- **Matplotlib** helps bring your analysis to life with insightful, easy-to-understand visualizations.
- Cleaning and analyzing data is just the first step—visualization is crucial for making your findings accessible to others.

With this knowledge, you can now confidently tackle more complex data analysis projects. By mastering these libraries and following the best practices outlined here, you'll be able to handle a wide variety of data challenges, from simple reports to advanced statistical analyses.

As you continue to work with Python, remember that practice is key. Keep experimenting with these techniques on different datasets, and soon you'll be uncovering valuable insights and telling compelling data-driven stories with ease.

Chapter 9: Python for AI and Machine Learning: A Beginner's Gateway

Artificial Intelligence (AI) and Machine Learning (ML) have revolutionized industries by enabling computers to learn from data, recognize patterns, and make decisions. Python, with its simplicity and powerful libraries, has become the preferred language for AI and ML development. This chapter introduces you to Python's role in AI and ML, foundational concepts, and practical steps to create your first machine learning model.

Why Python for AI and ML?

1. **Ease of Use**: Python's simple syntax reduces the learning curve for beginners.
2. **Extensive Libraries**: Libraries like scikit-learn, TensorFlow, and PyTorch offer robust tools for building ML models.
3. **Community Support**: A vast community ensures abundant tutorials, documentation, and problem-solving resources.
4. **Scalability**: Python adapts well to both small-scale experiments and large-scale production systems.

Key Libraries for AI and ML

1. **NumPy**:
   - For numerical computations and array manipulation.
2. **Pandas**:
   - For data manipulation and preprocessing.
3. **Matplotlib/Seaborn**:

- For data visualization.

4. **scikit-learn**:
   - For machine learning algorithms and evaluation.

5. **TensorFlow/PyTorch**:
   - For deep learning models and neural networks.

Understanding Machine Learning

What is Machine Learning?

Machine Learning (ML) allows computers to learn from data, improving their performance over time without being explicitly programmed. There are three main types of ML:

1. **Supervised Learning:**
   - In this type of learning, a model is trained using labeled data (where the correct answers are already provided). The model learns to make predictions based on this data.
   - **Example:** Predicting house prices using features like size, location, and number of bedrooms.

2. **Unsupervised Learning:**
   - Here, the model finds patterns or structures in data without having predefined labels. It's like discovering hidden relationships within the data.
   - **Example:** Grouping customers based on purchasing behavior.

3. **Reinforcement Learning:**
   - This type involves learning through trial and error, where the model gets feedback in the form of rewards or penalties. It helps the model learn optimal strategies through interaction with its environment.

- o **Example:** Teaching a robot to navigate through a maze by rewarding it for correct moves.

Building Your First Machine Learning Model

Now, let's explore the process of building a basic machine learning model. Imagine you're predicting house prices based on features like the size of the house and the number of bedrooms.

1. **Install Libraries:** Before you start, you'll need some essential Python libraries like **NumPy**, **Pandas**, and **scikit-learn**. These help with data manipulation and model building.
2. **Import Libraries:** The next step is to import these libraries into your workspace.
3. **Load the Dataset:** For this project, you'll use a dataset containing house prices, with features like the size of the house and the number of bedrooms.
4. **Preprocess the Data:** This step involves separating the data into inputs (features) and outputs (target variable), such as the house price.
5. **Train the Model:** Using a technique like **Linear Regression**, you'll train the model to understand the relationship between the features (like size and bedrooms) and the price of the house.
6. **Make Predictions:** Once the model is trained, you can use it to predict house prices for new data, and evaluate how well it performs using metrics like **Mean Squared Error (MSE)**.
7. **Visualize Predictions:** After testing your model, you can plot the actual vs. predicted prices to see how accurate your model is in predicting house prices.

Exploring Unsupervised Learning

Unsupervised learning helps discover hidden patterns in data. Let's look at an example: **customer segmentation**. In this case, the model groups customers based on their age and income without knowing beforehand how these groups should be formed.

By applying a technique like **K-Means clustering**, you can divide customers into groups that share similar characteristics. Visualizing these groups in a plot helps reveal insights into your data.

Moving to Deep Learning

Deep Learning is a specialized area of machine learning that mimics the human brain using **neural networks**. These networks have multiple layers and are capable of processing vast amounts of data. **TensorFlow** and **Keras** are popular libraries for building these models.

For example, you could use a deep learning model to classify handwritten digits, such as those from the **MNIST** dataset. By building and training a deep neural network, the model learns to recognize digits by processing images of handwritten numbers.

Best Practices for Beginners

1. **Start Simple:** Begin with basic models like **Linear Regression** and **Decision Trees** to grasp the core concepts.
2. **Clean Your Data:** Ensure your data is complete, consistent, and formatted correctly before feeding it into a model.
3. **Understand Metrics:** Learn about metrics such as **Mean Squared Error (MSE)** for regression and **Accuracy** for classification, which help evaluate model performance.

4. **Experiment and Iterate:** Don't be afraid to try different algorithms and fine-tune your model's parameters to improve performance.
5. **Use Prebuilt Datasets:** Explore free datasets available on platforms like **Kaggle** to practice and learn from real-world data.

Simplifying Complex AI Concepts for Beginners

AI and machine learning can seem daunting with terms like **neural networks**, **supervised learning**, and **backpropagation**. Let's break them down into easy-to-understand concepts:

1. **What is AI?** Artificial Intelligence is the science of teaching machines to think and act like humans. It's behind everyday systems, like Netflix recommending movies, or even self-driving cars making decisions on the road.
   - ○ **Analogy:** AI is like teaching a child to recognize different animals. You show them pictures of dogs and cats repeatedly, and they learn to identify these animals independently.
2. **Machine Learning: Teaching Machines to Learn** ML is a subset of AI that enables machines to learn from data. Instead of being programmed with specific instructions, the machine improves its ability to predict or make decisions by learning from past data.
   - ○ **Analogy:** It's like training a chef who gets better at cooking by following recipes, but over time, they stop needing the recipes and can cook from memory.
3. **Types of Machine Learning:**
   - ○ **Supervised Learning:** A teacher provides answers (labels) so the model can learn to make predictions.

- Unsupervised Learning: The model discovers patterns by itself without being told what to look for.
- Reinforcement Learning: The model learns by receiving rewards or penalties based on its actions.

4. **Neural Networks: The Brain of AI** Neural networks are algorithms inspired by the brain. They process data through layers of nodes (neurons) and learn to make predictions based on patterns.
   - **Analogy:** Think of it like an assembly line where raw materials (data) go in, workers (neurons) process them, and finished products (predictions) come out.

5. **Backpropagation: The Learning Process** Backpropagation is how a neural network improves by adjusting its internal settings (weights) to minimize errors.
   - **Analogy:** It's like playing darts—if you miss the bullseye, you adjust your aim and try again, getting closer to the target over time.

6. **Deep Learning: Scaling Up Neural Networks** Deep Learning uses large neural networks to solve complex tasks, like recognizing faces or translating languages.
   - **Analogy:** Deep learning is like assembling a team of experts, each working on a specific aspect of the task, to solve a complicated problem.

7. **Natural Language Processing (NLP): Teaching Machines to Understand Language** NLP allows machines to understand and respond to human language, like how chatbots or voice assistants work.
   - **Analogy:** Teaching a tourist a new language, where they learn words, context, and eventually can hold conversations.

8. **Computer Vision: Machines That See** Computer Vision enables machines to process and interpret visual data, such as images or videos.

o **Analogy:** It's like training a person to recognize objects in photos—showing them many labeled images to help them identify objects in new ones.

Key AI Techniques:

- **Decision Trees:** Making decisions by asking a series of questions, like playing "20 Questions."
- **Clustering:** Grouping similar data points together, like sorting laundry by color.
- **Recommendation Systems:** Suggesting products based on past preferences, like a waiter recommending dishes based on your previous orders.

Overcoming Common Beginner Challenges

1. **Overwhelming Terminology:** Simplify by using analogies and starting with basic projects.
2. **Large Datasets:** Use preprocessed datasets to practice.
3. **Algorithm Selection:** Begin with simple models like **Linear Regression** and **Decision Trees** to get comfortable with the basics.

A Beginner-Friendly AI Project

Project: Predicting House Prices with Linear Regression

- **Goal:** Use features like house size and number of bedrooms to predict prices.
- **Dataset:** A simple set of house features and prices.
- **Tools:** Use **scikit-learn** to build the model.

By breaking down AI concepts into simple analogies and practical projects, you can make meaningful progress in your journey toward understanding machine learning and artificial intelligence. With continued practice and experimentation, you'll be well on your way to becoming proficient in this exciting field!

Chapter 10: Debugging and Optimization: Writing Perfect Code

Debugging and optimization are essential skills for writing efficient, reliable, and maintainable code. Debugging helps identify and fix errors, while optimization improves the performance and scalability of your programs. This chapter delves into debugging techniques, optimization strategies, and tools that make your Python code error-free and efficient.

Understanding Debugging

Debugging is the process of identifying and resolving errors (bugs) in your code. Bugs can arise from syntax errors, logical errors, or runtime exceptions.

Common Types of Bugs

1. **Syntax Errors**:
    - Issues in code structure, such as missing colons or parentheses.
    - Example: print("Hello World" (missing closing parenthesis).
2. **Logical Errors**:
    - The code runs but produces incorrect results due to flawed logic.
    - Example: Using + instead of * in a formula.
3. **Runtime Errors**:
    - Errors that occur while the program is running, such as dividing by zero or accessing an undefined variable.

Debugging Techniques

1. **Print Statements**:
   - A simple yet effective debugging method is inserting print statements at various points in your code. This allows you to track the values of variables and understand the flow of the program.
2. **Python Debugger (pdb)**:
   - Python's built-in debugger, pdb, allows you to pause your program and step through it line by line. You can inspect variables and control the execution flow, making it easier to identify where things go wrong.
3. **Logging**:
   - The logging module enables more structured debugging. By logging important information at different points in your program, you can track the behavior and find issues without disrupting the flow. You can also set different logging levels (like DEBUG, INFO, or ERROR) to control the verbosity of the messages.
4. **IDE Debugging Tools**:
   - Integrated Development Environments (IDEs) like PyCharm and Visual Studio Code offer advanced debugging features. You can set breakpoints, step through your code, and inspect variables in real-time. These tools provide a more visual and intuitive way to identify issues compared to manual methods like print statements.

Debugging Workflow

1. **Reproduce the Bug**:
   - To begin debugging, you need to reliably reproduce the error. Understanding the steps

that lead to the issue helps narrow down the problem.

2. **Isolate the Problem**:
   - Once the issue is reproducible, focus on isolating the specific section of code where the error occurs. This can involve commenting out sections of code or using tools to step through the program.

3. **Analyze the Code**:
   - After isolating the problem, analyze your code carefully. Look for common issues like off-by-one errors, logic mistakes, or incorrect assumptions that may have led to the bug.

4. **Fix the Issue**:
   - Apply the necessary fix to the code, then test it thoroughly to ensure the problem is resolved.

5. **Prevent Future Bugs**:
   - After fixing the bug, consider adding additional tests or input validations to prevent similar issues from arising in the future.

Optimizing Python Code

Optimization focuses on making your code more efficient, whether that's through improving speed, memory usage, or scalability.

1. **Performance Bottlenecks**:
   - Identify areas where your program is slow or inefficient. Tools like profiling can help pinpoint the exact lines of code that are causing delays.

2. **Optimization Techniques**:
   - **Efficient Data Structures**: Choosing the right data structure can greatly improve performance. For example, using sets for membership checks is faster than using lists.

- List Comprehensions: Replacing loops with list comprehensions can make your code both more concise and efficient.
- **Use Built-In Functions**: Python's built-in functions are highly optimized. Leveraging them, instead of writing custom loops, can significantly boost performance.
- **Avoid Recomputing**: If a value is calculated multiple times, consider storing it in a variable or using a caching mechanism to avoid redundant work.
- **Vectorized Operations**: For large datasets, libraries like NumPy allow you to perform operations on arrays in a more efficient way, rather than using loops.
- **Minimize I/O Operations**: Reading or writing to files or databases can slow down your program. Batch operations together to minimize I/O.

3. **Memory Optimization**:
   - **Use Generators**: Generators are memory-efficient because they yield items one at a time, rather than storing everything in memory at once.
   - **Avoid Large Temporary Variables**: Whenever possible, try to process data in-place to save memory.
   - **Release Unused Memory**: Make sure to delete variables that are no longer needed to free up memory.

Debugging and Optimization Tools

Debugging Tools:

- **pdb**: A built-in debugger for stepping through code and inspecting variables.

- **PyCharm/VS Code Debugger**: Advanced IDE debuggers that offer features like breakpoints, variable inspection, and step-by-step code execution.
- **Logging**: Helps keep track of runtime information for debugging purposes.
- **Traceback**: Analyze the error messages from a stack trace to locate the issue.

Optimization Tools:

- **cProfile**: Helps identify performance bottlenecks by profiling the code execution.
- **timeit**: Measures the execution time of code snippets to compare performance.
- **line_profiler**: Profiles the execution time of individual lines in your code.
- **memory_profiler**: Analyzes memory usage to optimize resource consumption.

Best Practices

1. **Write Tests**:
    - Implement unit tests to catch bugs early in the development process and prevent regressions.
2. **Iterate on Optimization**:
    - Focus on optimizing the areas of your code that are causing performance bottlenecks. Don't prematurely optimize code that doesn't need improvement.
3. **Document Code**:
    - Write clear comments to explain complex logic. This will help in debugging later on and make the code more maintainable.
4. **Refactor Regularly**:
    - Continuously improve your code to maintain readability and performance. Don't let your codebase become cluttered with workarounds and hacks.

5. **Learn from Errors**:
   - ○ Take note of recurring bugs or issues and update your processes to prevent them in the future.

Debugging Tools in PyCharm and VS Code

Both **PyCharm** and **VS Code** offer robust debugging tools that can help developers resolve issues efficiently.

- **PyCharm** provides a range of features like breakpoints, variable inspection, and inline debugging, which make it highly intuitive for debugging. The IDE also supports features such as exception breakpoints, which automatically pause execution when an exception is thrown.
- **VS Code**, on the other hand, is lightweight and highly customizable. It also supports debugging with breakpoints and allows developers to log values dynamically without changing the code using logpoints.

Both tools offer step functions like "step into," "step over," and "step out," allowing you to control the execution flow. Depending on your needs, you can choose the tool that best fits your workflow.

Best Practices for Debugging

1. **Understand the Problem**:
   - ○ Reproduce the error consistently before trying to fix it. This ensures you're addressing the right issue.
2. **Use IDE Tools**:
   - ○ Leverage the advanced debugging tools in PyCharm and VS Code to inspect variables, set breakpoints, and step through your code.
3. **Divide and Conquer**:

- Break down your code to isolate the specific part causing the issue.
4. **Read Error Messages Carefully**:
   - Stack traces and error messages provide valuable clues. Understanding these will help you pinpoint the source of the problem.
5. **Write Tests**:
   - Use unit tests to ensure your code is working as expected and to catch bugs early in the development process.
6. **Optimize Debugging Time**:
   - Use the right debugging tools and techniques to save time and focus on resolving issues quickly.

Conclusion

Mastering the art of debugging and optimization is crucial for any developer. Whether you're identifying the root cause of an issue or refining your code to perform at its best, having a structured approach will save you valuable time and energy. Through tools like print statements, debuggers, and logging, you can systematically track down errors and gain insights into your program's behavior. And by applying optimization techniques such as using efficient data structures, minimizing redundant calculations, and leveraging memory-efficient approaches, you can ensure that your code runs smoothly and effectively.

Remember that debugging is not just about fixing issues—it's also about learning from your mistakes and continuously improving your workflow. The more you debug, the better you'll become at spotting potential problems before they arise. Similarly, optimization should be an ongoing process, where you strive to make your code cleaner, faster, and more maintainable.

By incorporating these best practices into your development routine, you'll be able to write robust, high-performance Python code that's not only functional but also scalable and efficient. Keep refining your debugging and optimization skills, and always strive for code that's as efficient and error-free as possible.

Chapter 11: Crafting Your Python Portfolio

A strong portfolio is essential for showcasing your Python skills and standing out in a competitive job market. Whether you're a beginner looking for your first job or an experienced developer aiming to advance your career, a well-crafted portfolio demonstrates your expertise, problem-solving abilities, and creativity. This chapter provides a step-by-step guide to building a compelling Python portfolio that captures attention and highlights your unique skills.

Why a Python Portfolio Matters

A Python portfolio serves as tangible evidence of your abilities, offering several benefits:

- **Showcases Your Skills**: Demonstrates your proficiency in Python and its libraries.
- **Proves Problem-Solving Abilities**: Highlights how you approach and solve real-world problems.
- **Builds Credibility**: Sets you apart by showing practical experience beyond a resume.
- **Engages Employers and Clients**: Provides a visual and interactive way for recruiters to assess your skills.

Components of a Strong Python Portfolio

Your portfolio should be comprehensive yet concise. Key components include:

1. **Introduction**:

- A brief overview of who you are, your skills, and your career goals.
- Example: "I am a Python developer passionate about data analysis, machine learning, and automation. My projects showcase innovative solutions to real-world challenges."

2. **Featured Projects**:
   - Highlight 3–5 diverse projects that demonstrate your expertise.
   - Include a short description, technologies used, and links to live demos or repositories.
3. **Skills Section**:
   - List Python libraries and frameworks you've mastered (e.g., Pandas, Flask, TensorFlow).
4. **Code Repository**:
   - Link to your GitHub or GitLab profile to showcase your code.
5. **Contact Information**:
   - Provide links to your LinkedIn profile, email, or personal website.

Steps to Build Your Python Portfolio

Step 1: Identify Your Niche

Focus on an area of Python that aligns with your career goals. Popular niches include:

- **Web Development**: Flask, Django.
- **Data Analysis and Visualization**: Pandas, Matplotlib, Seaborn.
- **Machine Learning**: Scikit-learn, TensorFlow, PyTorch.
- **Automation**: Selenium, PyAutoGUI.
- **Game Development**: Pygame.

Step 2: Choose Projects That Showcase Your Skills

Select projects that demonstrate your problem-solving abilities and technical knowledge. Here are some project ideas:

1. **Web Development**:
   - A blog platform using Flask or Django.
   - A personal portfolio website showcasing your projects.
2. **Data Analysis**:
   - Analyze and visualize COVID-19 trends using Pandas and Matplotlib.
   - Build a dashboard for financial data visualization.
3. **Machine Learning**:
   - Predict house prices using Scikit-learn.
   - Create a sentiment analysis tool for social media comments.
4. **Automation**:
   - Develop a script to automate email notifications.
   - Build a web scraper to gather data from e-commerce websites.
5. **Game Development**:
   - Design a basic game like Snake or Tic-Tac-Toe using Pygame.

Step 3: Document Your Projects

Provide context for each project:

1. **Problem Statement**:
   - Clearly define the problem your project solves.

- Example: "Built a recommendation system to suggest movies based on user preferences."

2. **Technology Stack**:
   - List the Python libraries, frameworks, and tools used.
   - Example: "Flask for web development, SQLite for database management."

3. **Process**:
   - Briefly explain your development process, challenges faced, and how you resolved them.

4. **Results**:
   - Highlight measurable outcomes.
   - Example: "Reduced data processing time by 30% using optimized Pandas operations."

Step 4: Organize Your Portfolio

Structure your portfolio for easy navigation. A simple layout might include:

1. **Home Page**: Introduce yourself.
2. **Projects Page**: Showcase detailed case studies of your projects.
3. **Skills Page**: Highlight your technical abilities.
4. **Contact Page**: Provide contact information.

Tools for Building Your Portfolio
1. GitHub/GitLab

- Use GitHub to host your code and provide version control.
- Create a professional README for each project.

2. Personal Website

- Build a custom portfolio site using:
    - **Flask/Django**: For dynamic content.
    - **HTML/CSS**: For design and layout.
    - **GitHub Pages**: For free hosting.

3. Jupyter Notebooks

- Showcase data analysis or machine learning projects interactively.
- Example: Use Jupyter notebooks to visualize datasets with code snippets.

4. Online Platforms

- **LinkedIn**: Add portfolio links to your profile.
- **Kaggle**: Share data science projects and compete in challenges.
- **Medium**: Publish blog posts explaining your projects.

Example Portfolio Project

Project Title: Movie Recommendation System
Objective: Build a recommendation system to suggest movies based on user preferences.

Steps:

1. **Define the Problem**:
    - Help users discover movies they'll love based on ratings.
2. **Collect Data**:

- Use a publicly available dataset (e.g., MovieLens).

3. **Process the Data**:
   - Clean and preprocess the dataset using Pandas.
4. **Build the Model**:
   - Implement collaborative filtering using Scikit-learn.
5. **Evaluate and Visualize**:
   - Measure model accuracy and visualize recommendations.
6. **Document Results**:
   - Share insights, challenges, and future improvements.

Technologies Used:

- Pandas, Scikit-learn, Matplotlib, Flask.

Output:

- A web app where users can input their movie preferences and get personalized recommendations.

11.6 Best Practices for a Winning Portfolio

1. **Focus on Quality Over Quantity**:
   - It's better to have 3 polished projects than 10 incomplete ones.
2. **Keep It Updated**:
   - Regularly add new projects to showcase your growth.
3. **Make It Accessible**:
   - Ensure links and demos work flawlessly.

4. **Use Clear Communication**:
    - Write concise, engaging descriptions of your projects.
5. **Tailor It to Your Audience**:
    - Customize your portfolio to target specific job roles or industries.

11.7 Promoting Your Portfolio

- **LinkedIn**: Share updates about your projects.
- **Open Source Contributions**: Contribute to popular Python repositories.
- **Networking**: Share your portfolio with peers, mentors, and potential employers.
- **Interviews**: Use your portfolio as a talking point during technical interviews.

Creating an Impressive Portfolio to Showcase Your Python Skills

An impressive portfolio can be the key to standing out in the competitive field of Python programming. It's more than just a collection of projects—it's a testament to your expertise, creativity, and problem-solving abilities. This guide walks you through creating a portfolio that effectively highlights your Python skills, captivates employers, and serves as a powerful tool for career advancement.

1. Why a Portfolio is Essential for Python Programmers

Your portfolio:

- **Demonstrates Practical Skills**: Shows that you can apply Python concepts to solve real-world problems.

- **Builds Credibility**: Provides tangible evidence of your expertise.
- **Reflects Professionalism**: Highlights your ability to document, organize, and present work.
- **Engages Potential Employers**: Offers a visual and interactive way to evaluate your capabilities.

2. Elements of an Impressive Python Portfolio

To create a well-rounded portfolio, include the following components:

2.1 Introduction

- Write a brief, engaging bio.
- Highlight your career goals and key strengths.
- Example:
  "Hi, I'm Alex, a Python developer specializing in data analysis and machine learning. I create impactful solutions that drive insights and innovation. My portfolio reflects my passion for problem-solving and my commitment to coding excellence."

2.2 Featured Projects

- Showcase 3–5 standout projects that demonstrate your versatility.
- Include:
  - A **problem statement**: What problem did the project solve?
  - The **technology stack**: Python libraries, frameworks, and tools used.
  - Key **features** or results.

2.3 Skills Section

- Clearly list your technical expertise, including:
    - Python libraries: Pandas, NumPy, TensorFlow, Flask.
    - Frameworks: Django, FastAPI.
    - Tools: Git, Jupyter Notebooks, Docker.

2.4 Code Repository

- Link to your GitHub or GitLab profile.
- Organize repositories by projects, using descriptive READMEs to explain:
    - Project purpose.
    - Installation and usage instructions.
    - Key highlights.

2.5 Contact Information

- Include:
    - Professional email address.
    - LinkedIn profile.
    - Personal website or portfolio link.

3. Steps to Build Your Python Portfolio
3.1 Choose a Niche

Align your projects with your career aspirations:

- **Web Development**: Flask or Django apps.
- **Data Science**: Exploratory data analysis and visualization.
- **Machine Learning**: Predictive models and neural networks.

113

- **Automation**: Scripts for repetitive tasks.
- **Game Development**: Interactive games with Pygame.

3.2 Select and Build Projects

Choose projects that reflect diverse skills. Here are examples:

1. **Web Application**:
   - **Idea**: A task management tool.
   - **Stack**: Flask, SQLAlchemy, Bootstrap.
   - **Features**: User authentication, CRUD operations, and responsive design.
2. **Data Analysis**:
   - **Idea**: Analyzing global temperature trends.
   - **Stack**: Pandas, Matplotlib, Seaborn.
   - **Features**: Data cleaning, trend visualization, and actionable insights.
3. **Machine Learning Model**:
   - **Idea**: Predicting house prices.
   - **Stack**: Scikit-learn, NumPy.
   - **Features**: Regression model, feature engineering, and model evaluation.
4. **Automation Tool**:
   - **Idea**: A script to scrape and summarize news articles.
   - **Stack**: BeautifulSoup, Requests.
   - **Features**: Data extraction and text summarization.
5. **Interactive Game**:
   - **Idea**: A snake game.
   - **Stack**: Pygame.
   - **Features**: Dynamic gameplay and score tracking.

3.3 Document Your Projects

Documentation is key to making your portfolio professional and user-friendly.

1. **README Files**:
    *   Write detailed README files for each project in your repository.
    *   Include:
        *   Project overview.
        *   Setup instructions.
        *   Features and screenshots.
2. **Code Comments**:
    *   Use meaningful comments to explain your logic and enhance readability.
3. **Blog Posts**:
    *   Write about your projects to demonstrate communication skills.
    *   Example platforms: Medium, Dev.to.

3.4 Create a Personal Website

Build a dedicated website to host your portfolio.

1. **Tools**:
    *   **Static Site Generators**: Jekyll, Hugo.
    *   **Web Frameworks**: Flask, Django.
    *   **No-Code Platforms**: Squarespace, Wix.
2. **Structure**:
    *   **Home**: Brief introduction.
    *   **Projects**: Showcase case studies.
    *   **About**: Skills and bio.
    *   **Contact**: Links and form.
3. **Example Hosting**:

- **GitHub Pages**: Free hosting for static sites.
- **Heroku**: Deploy Flask or Django apps.

3.5 Use Jupyter Notebooks

For data-related projects, Jupyter Notebooks allow you to combine code, visuals, and narrative in a single document.

4. Designing an Eye-Catching Portfolio
4.1 Prioritize Usability

- Use a clean, intuitive design.
- Ensure easy navigation between projects.

4.2 Include Visuals

- Use screenshots, diagrams, and charts to enhance project descriptions.

4.3 Highlight Achievements

- Mention awards, certifications, or recognition.

4.4 Optimize for Mobile

- Ensure your website is responsive for mobile users.

5. Promote Your Portfolio
5.1 Share on LinkedIn

- Regularly post updates about new projects.

5.2 Contribute to Open Source

- Collaborate on Python repositories to showcase teamwork and expertise.

5.3 Participate in Competitions

- Enter hackathons or Kaggle challenges and include results in your portfolio.

5.4 Network

- Share your portfolio with peers, mentors, and industry professionals.

6. Example Portfolio Layout
Homepage:

- Welcome message and brief introduction.

Projects Page:

- Interactive cards for each project with links to live demos and code.

About Page:

- Highlight skills, experience, and career goals.

Contact Page:

- Contact form, email, and LinkedIn links.

7. Best Practices for a Winning Portfolio

1. **Focus on Quality**:
   - Highlight your best work, even if it's just a few projects.
2. **Keep It Updated**:
   - Regularly add new projects or skills.
3. **Be Authentic**:
   - Let your portfolio reflect your personality and passion.
4. **Test Everything**:
   - Ensure links, demos, and features work flawlessly.
5. **Tailor It**:
   - Adapt your portfolio for different roles or industries.

Providing Templates for Project Documentation and GitHub Repositories

Well-documented projects and organized GitHub repositories demonstrate professionalism and make your work accessible to potential employers, collaborators, and clients. This section provides templates and guidelines to create clear, concise, and effective project documentation and GitHub repositories. We'll also include a guide to prepare for Python-related job interviews.

As we wrap up this chapter, it's important to remember that effective project documentation and organization are key components to a successful development workflow. Clear, well-structured documentation not only makes it easier for others to understand and contribute to your project, but it also serves as a reference for your future self when revisiting the project.

Using templates for your README.md, CONTRIBUTING.md, and issue reports ensures that your project is easy to navigate and understand. These templates provide a consistent, professional structure that saves time and promotes collaboration. Similarly, organizing your GitHub repository with descriptive commit messages and a logical folder structure can streamline your development process and improve team collaboration.

As for preparing for Python-related job interviews, the process is multifaceted. By focusing on core Python skills, brushing up on algorithms, and practicing with real-world projects, you will be better equipped to showcase your abilities and stand out in interviews. Remember, job interviews often go beyond technical expertise—they also test your problem-solving, communication, and teamwork skills.

Whether you're preparing for a new project or a career shift, these best practices will set you on the path to success. Keep refining your skills, and don't hesitate to take the next step—whether it's contributing to an open-source project or tackling your dream job. The journey of learning and growing as a developer never truly ends!

Chapter 12: Beyond the Basics: Continuing Your Python Journey

Mastering Python basics is just the beginning of an exciting journey. As you advance, you'll discover a universe of opportunities to deepen your expertise and expand your skill set. Whether you're interested in developing complex applications, exploring data science, or diving into machine learning, this chapter offers a roadmap to continue your Python journey beyond the basics.

Advanced Python Concepts

Object-Oriented Programming (OOP)

- **Inheritance**: Allows you to reuse code across related classes. For example, a base Vehicle class can share common attributes with a derived Car class.
- **Polymorphism**: Enables creating methods that work across different class types, ensuring flexibility in your code.
- **Encapsulation**: Protects data by restricting access to internal methods and attributes, fostering better control and modularity.

Decorators

- Modify the behavior of functions or methods without altering their structure. Think of them as wrappers that add functionality, like converting a string to uppercase automatically in a greeting function.

Generators and Iterators

- **Generators**: Yield items one at a time, making them memory-efficient for handling large datasets. For instance, generating Fibonacci numbers on-the-fly without storing the entire sequence.
- **Iterators**: Provide a standard way to traverse through items in a collection, such as looping through a list.

Context Managers

- Simplify resource management using the with statement. For example, reading a file ensures it's closed automatically when the task is complete.

Advanced Libraries and Frameworks

Web Development

1. **Flask**: A lightweight framework ideal for small to medium web applications. Its flexibility makes it perfect for quick prototypes or simpler websites.
2. **Django**: A full-stack framework packed with tools like database management, authentication, and a robust admin panel. It's well-suited for large, scalable projects.

Data Science

1. **Pandas**: Streamlines data manipulation, allowing for tasks like cleaning and analyzing data tables effortlessly.
2. **Matplotlib**: A go-to tool for creating plots and visualizations, such as line graphs or bar charts.

Machine Learning

1. **Scikit-learn**: Simplifies tasks like classification and regression with user-friendly APIs for building and training machine learning models.

2. **TensorFlow**: Powers deep learning by providing tools to create and train neural networks for advanced applications like image recognition.

Building Real-World Applications

Portfolio Projects

- **Web Applications**: Build blogs or e-commerce platforms using Flask or Django.
- **Data Dashboards**: Create interactive dashboards with tools like Dash or Plotly.
- **Automation Scripts**: Develop tools for web scraping or automating repetitive tasks.

Open Source Contributions

- Collaborate on projects hosted on GitHub to improve your skills and connect with the coding community.

Python Specializations

Data Engineering

- Utilize libraries like Apache Airflow for orchestrating workflows or Pandas and SQLAlchemy for ETL (Extract, Transform, Load) pipelines.

DevOps

- Automate deployment pipelines with Docker, integrating Python for scripting and configuration management.

Game Development

- Explore interactive game creation using Pygame, a library designed for game development.

Staying Updated and Motivated

Following Industry Trends

- Stay informed about Python updates and emerging libraries by following blogs like Real Python or Towards Data Science.

Participating in Coding Challenges

- Platforms like LeetCode or Codewars provide daily challenges to keep your skills sharp.

Joining Python Communities

- Engage in forums like Reddit's r/Python or participate in Python meetups to network and learn.

Building Expertise in Python

Certifications

- Pursue certifications like Microsoft's Python for Data Science or AWS Developer credentials to validate your skills.

Mentoring

- Teaching others Python reinforces your own understanding while helping others grow.

Beyond Programming

- Apply Python to niche fields like IoT (Internet of Things), robotics, or blockchain development to expand your horizons.

Advanced Topics in Python

Web Development

- Master frameworks like Flask and Django, diving deeper into features like modular application design, middleware integration, or query optimization.
- Build APIs with tools like FastAPI, implementing features like authentication using OAuth2 or JWT.

API Integration

- Learn to interact with third-party APIs, enabling functionalities like payment processing or real-time data retrieval.
- Build robust APIs with rate-limiting and error-handling mechanisms for better scalability and reliability.

Advanced Data Science

- Handle large datasets with PySpark or Dask to perform parallel computations efficiently.
- Use machine learning pipelines to streamline workflows, employing libraries like Scikit-learn or TensorFlow for deep learning tasks.
- Create interactive visualizations or analyze geographical data using Dash or geopandas.

By mastering these advanced concepts, you'll unlock Python's full potential, positioning yourself for success in various industries and innovative projects.

Python for Emerging Technologies

4.1 Internet of Things (IoT)

- Use Python on Raspberry Pi for IoT projects.
- Libraries: GPIOZero, MQTT.

Blockchain

- Develop smart contracts using Python frameworks like web3.py.

Robotics

- Control robots using ROS (Robot Operating System).

Learning Resources
Online Platforms

- **FreeCodeCamp**: Tutorials for advanced web development.
- **Kaggle**: Data science challenges and datasets.

Books

- *Fluent Python* by Luciano Ramalho.
- *Deep Learning with Python* by François Chollet.

Communities

- Join forums like r/Python on Reddit.
- Attend Python meetups and conferences.

Recommend Books, Courses, and Communities for Continued Learning

Python's simplicity and versatility make it an excellent language for developers of all skill levels. However, staying competitive requires continuous learning. Books, courses, and communities provide invaluable resources to keep your skills sharp and stay updated on industry trends. This section recommends essential resources for Python learners, ranging from foundational knowledge to advanced applications.

1. Books for Continued Learning

1.1 Foundational Python Books

1. **"Python Crash Course" by Eric Matthes**:
   - A hands-on, project-based introduction to Python programming.
   - Ideal for beginners who want to build real-world projects quickly.
2. **"Automate the Boring Stuff with Python" by Al Sweigart**:
   - Focuses on automating everyday tasks like data organization, file management, and web scraping.
   - Great for practical, immediate applications.

1.2 Intermediate and Advanced Books

1. **"Fluent Python" by Luciano Ramalho**:
   - Explores Python's deeper features like data models, metaprogramming, and concurrency.
   - Perfect for experienced developers seeking mastery.
2. **"Effective Python: 90 Specific Ways to Write Better Python" by Brett Slatkin**:
   - Offers practical advice for writing efficient, maintainable, and Pythonic code.
3. **"Deep Learning with Python" by François Chollet**:
   - A comprehensive guide to deep learning using TensorFlow and Keras.
   - Best for learners venturing into AI and machine learning.

1.3 Specialized Python Books

1. **"Python for Data Analysis" by Wes McKinney**:
   - The definitive guide to data manipulation using Pandas and NumPy.
2. **"Test-Driven Development with Python" by Harry Percival**:
   - Focuses on building robust software through testing frameworks.
3. **"Black Hat Python: Python Programming for Hackers and Pentesters" by Justin Seitz**:
   - For those interested in cybersecurity and ethical hacking.

2. Online Courses for Python Enthusiasts

2.1 Beginner-Friendly Courses

1. **"Python for Everybody" by Dr. Charles Severance (Coursera)**:
   - An introductory series covering Python basics and web scraping.
   - Available for free with an optional paid certificate.
2. **"The Complete Python Bootcamp" by Jose Portilla (Udemy)**:
   - A popular, comprehensive course covering Python 3 from beginner to advanced topics.

2.2 Intermediate and Advanced Courses

- **"Python Data Science Handbook" by Jake VanderPlas (O'Reilly)**:
  - Includes hands-on tutorials for using Python in data science workflows.

- **"CS50's Introduction to Artificial Intelligence with Python" (edX)**:
  - Teaches AI concepts and their implementation in Python, including search algorithms and machine learning.
- **"Python for Finance" by Yves Hilpisch (Udemy)**:
  - Focuses on using Python for financial analysis, modeling, and algorithmic trading.

2.3 Free Resources

1. **Kaggle**:
   - Offers Python tutorials and interactive projects tailored to data science.
2. **Real Python**:
   - Free tutorials and guides on various Python topics, from beginner to advanced levels.
3. **Google's Python Class**:
   - A free class for people with some programming experience, covering Python basics and beyond.

3. Communities for Networking and Learning
3.1 Online Forums

1. **Reddit (r/Python)**:
   - A vibrant community for Python enthusiasts to discuss trends, projects, and solutions.
2. **Stack Overflow**:
   - A Q&A platform where developers troubleshoot coding issues and share knowledge.

3.2 Social Media and Chat Platforms

1. **Python Discord**:
   - Offers channels for Python discussions, project collaboration, and career advice.
2. **Twitter**:
   - Follow hashtags like #Python and accounts like @ThePSF (Python Software Foundation) for news and tips.

3.3 Professional Communities

1. **PyCon Conferences**:
   - Annual Python conferences provide workshops, keynotes, and networking opportunities.
2. **Local Meetups**:
   - Join local Python meetups through Meetup.com to connect with developers in your area.
3. **LinkedIn Groups**:
   - Groups like "Python Developers" offer discussions, job postings, and insights.

3.4 Open Source Platforms

1. **GitHub**:
   - Explore repositories, contribute to open-source projects, and collaborate with other developers.
2. **Kaggle**:
   - Participate in data science competitions to test and enhance your Python skills.

Motivational Conclusion: The Endless Opportunities Python Opens Up

Python is more than a programming language—it's a gateway to endless opportunities. Its versatility empowers you to explore diverse fields like web development, data science, machine learning, robotics, and even space exploration. By mastering Python, you gain the tools to transform ideas into reality, solve real-world problems, and innovate in ways that make an impact.

As you continue your Python journey:

- **Be Curious**: Challenge yourself with new projects, domains, and concepts.
- **Stay Persistent**: Remember, every expert was once a beginner.
- **Engage with the Community**: Surround yourself with like-minded learners and professionals who inspire growth.

Python's potential is limitless, and so is yours. Whether you're creating the next groundbreaking AI, developing a game that captures imaginations, or building tools that simplify lives, Python is your ally. Your journey is unique, your contributions are valuable, and your future is bright. Keep learning, keep coding, and embrace the endless opportunities Python offers. The only limit is your imagination.

Conclusion

As we reach the end of this book, it's clear that Python is much more than a programming language—it's a tool for creativity, innovation, and problem-solving. Whether you're a beginner just starting your journey or an experienced developer looking to refine your skills, Python offers something for everyone. Its versatility, simplicity, and vast ecosystem make it the perfect language to explore a wide range of fields, from web development to data science, automation, artificial intelligence, and beyond.

Throughout this book, you've learned not just the fundamentals of Python, but also how to apply it to real-world problems, build impactful projects, and craft a professional portfolio that showcases your skills. You've been introduced to debugging techniques, optimization strategies, and advanced topics that open up new dimensions of programming.

But this is just the beginning. Python is a living, evolving language with a vibrant community that continually pushes the boundaries of what's possible. By continuing to learn, practice, and explore, you'll unlock even more opportunities to innovate, create, and make a meaningful impact.

Your Journey Ahead

1. **Experiment and Build**: Start new projects that challenge you and deepen your understanding.
2. **Engage and Collaborate**: Join Python communities, contribute to open-source projects, and network with other developers.

3. **Stay Curious**: Explore advanced concepts, new libraries, and emerging trends in Python.

A Final Note

The world of programming is vast and ever-changing, and Python is your gateway to endless possibilities. Whether you dream of building groundbreaking AI models, simplifying lives through automation, or solving the world's biggest challenges with data, Python equips you with the skills to turn your vision into reality.

Embrace the journey ahead with confidence, curiosity, and determination. The possibilities are limitless, and your potential is boundless. Keep learning, keep coding, and let Python be the tool that brings your ideas to life. Your future as a Python developer is bright—now go out and create something extraordinary!

References

Below is a comprehensive list of resources, books, and tools referenced throughout this book. These materials provide additional insights and opportunities to deepen your knowledge of Python and its applications.

Books

1. Matthes, Eric. *Python Crash Course: A Hands-On, Project-Based Introduction to Programming*. No Starch Press, 2019.
2. Sweigart, Al. *Automate the Boring Stuff with Python*. No Starch Press, 2020.
3. Ramalho, Luciano. *Fluent Python: Clear, Concise, and Effective Programming*. O'Reilly Media, 2022.
4. Slatkin, Brett. *Effective Python: 90 Specific Ways to Write Better Python*. Addison-Wesley, 2020.
5. Chollet, François. *Deep Learning with Python*. Manning Publications, 2021.
6. McKinney, Wes. *Python for Data Analysis: Data Wrangling with Pandas, NumPy, and IPython*. O'Reilly Media, 2018.

Online Courses

1. Severance, Dr. Charles. "Python for Everybody." Coursera.
   https://www.coursera.org/specializations/python
2. Portilla, Jose. "The Complete Python Bootcamp." Udemy.
   https://www.udemy.com/course/complete-python-bootcamp

3. Harvard University. "CS50's Introduction to Artificial Intelligence with Python." edX. https://cs50.harvard.edu/ai/

Libraries and Tools

1. Python Software Foundation. Python Documentation. https://docs.python.org/3/
2. Pandas Documentation. https://pandas.pydata.org/docs/
3. Flask Documentation. https://flask.palletsprojects.com/en/latest/
4. TensorFlow Documentation. https://www.tensorflow.org/
5. Scikit-learn Documentation. https://scikit-learn.org/stable/
6. Docker Documentation. https://docs.docker.com/

Online Communities

1. Reddit Python Community (r/Python). https://www.reddit.com/r/Python/
2. Stack Overflow. Python Questions and Answers. https://stackoverflow.com/questions/tagged/python
3. Python Discord. https://pythondiscord.com/
4. Kaggle. Data Science Competitions and Datasets. https://www.kaggle.com/

Additional Resources

1. Real Python Tutorials. https://realpython.com/

2. Google's Python Class.
   https://developers.google.com/edu/python
3. GitHub. Explore Open-Source Python Projects.
   https://github.com/topics/python
4. Medium Articles on Python Development.
   https://medium.com/tag/python
5. Towards Data Science. Tutorials and Articles on Data Science and Python.
   https://towardsdatascience.com/

About the Author

Dr. Evelyn Harper is a passionate software developer, data scientist, and educator with over a decade of experience in programming and teaching Python to learners worldwide. Known for her ability to simplify complex concepts, Dr. Harper has dedicated her career to making programming accessible to beginners while providing advanced insights for seasoned developers.

After earning her PhD in Computer Science from the University of Cambridge, Dr. Harper worked as a data scientist for leading tech companies, where she specialized in machine learning, automation, and data analysis. Her innovative projects include developing scalable AI models for healthcare and designing automation tools that save hours of manual work across industries.

Beyond her professional achievements, Dr. Harper is a sought-after speaker at international conferences such as PyCon and Data Science Global. She also serves as a mentor to aspiring programmers, encouraging them to embrace challenges and continuously learn.

In addition to her technical expertise, Dr. Harper is an advocate for diversity in tech. She actively works to create opportunities for underrepresented groups to pursue careers in programming and data science.

When she's not coding or teaching, Dr. Harper enjoys writing about emerging trends in Python, contributing to open-source projects, and exploring the intersection of technology and art.

Why This Book?

With *[Python Programming]*, Dr. Evelyn Harper combines her love for Python and her commitment to education. The book is designed to guide readers from foundational concepts to advanced applications, empowering them to build impactful projects and achieve their goals. Whether you're a beginner or an experienced programmer, Dr. Harper's engaging approach ensures you'll discover new opportunities to grow and thrive in the ever-evolving world of Python programming.

Copyright Notice

www.ingramcontent.com/pod-product-compliance
Lightning Source LLC
LaVergne TN
LVHW051245050326
832903LV00028B/2578